Ultimate Skiing

Ron LeMaster

Human Kinetics

Library of Congress Cataloging-in-Publication Data

LeMaster, Ron, 1949-
  Ultimate skiing / Ron LeMaster.
      p. cm.
  Includes index.
  ISBN-13: 978-0-7360-7959-4 (soft cover)
  ISBN-10: 0-7360-7959-9 (soft cover)
  1. Skis and skiing. I. Title.
  GV854.L455 2009
  796.93--dc22
                          2009025545

ISBN-10: 0-7360-7959-9 (print)   ISBN-10: 0-7360-8621-8 (Adobe PDF)
ISBN-13: 978-0-7360-7959-4 (print)   ISBN-13: 978-0-7360-8621-9 (Adobe PDF)

This book is a revised edition of *The Skier's Edge* published in 1999 by Human Kinetics.

Acquisitions Editor: Laurel Plotzke; **Developmental Editor:** Mandy Eastin-Allen; **Assistant Editor:** Laura Podeschi; **Copyeditor:** John Wentworth; **Indexer:** Betty Frizzéll; **Graphic Designer:** Robert Reuther; **Cover Designer:** Keith Blomberg; **Photographer (cover and interior):** Ron LeMaster, unless otherwise noted; **Photo Production Manager:** Jason Allen; **Art Manager:** Kelly Hendren; **Associate Art Manager:** Alan L. Wilborn; **Illustrator:** Ron LeMaster, unless otherwise noted. Illustrations on pages 22, 26, 78, 79, 84, 92, 93 (figure 6.8), and 100 © Joyce Mihran Turley; **Printer:** Premier Print Group

Human Kinetics books are available at special discounts for bulk purchase. Special editions or book excerpts can also be created to specification. For details, contact the Special Sales Manager at Human Kinetics.

Printed in the United States of America   10 9 8 7 6 5 4 3 2 1

Human Kinetics
Web site: www.HumanKinetics.com

United States: Human Kinetics
P.O. Box 5076
Champaign, IL 61825-5076
800-747-4457
e-mail: humank@hkusa.com

Canada: Human Kinetics
475 Devonshire Road Unit 100
Windsor, ON N8Y 2L5
800-465-7301 (in Canada only)
e-mail: info@hkcanada.com

Europe: Human Kinetics
107 Bradford Road
Stanningley
Leeds LS28 6AT, United Kingdom
+44 (0) 113 255 5665
e-mail: hk@hkeurope.com

Australia: Human Kinetics
57A Price Avenue
Lower Mitcham, South Australia 5062
08 8372 0999
e-mail: info@hkaustralia.com

New Zealand: Human Kinetics
Division of Sports Distributors NZ Ltd.
P.O. Box 300 226 Albany
North Shore City
Auckland
0064 9 448 1207
e-mail: info@humankinetics.co.nz

E4686

This book is dedicated to Curt Chase.

Contents

Preface

In 1998 I wrote a book called *The Skier's Edge*. It was published just as the ski world was discovering what have come to be known as shaped skis. Since then, the sport has gone through something of a revolution. Our skis are now cut with an accentuated hourglass shape whose curvature has a radius that is typically 60 percent smaller than their predecessors, and are roughly 15 percent shorter. As a result, everyone skis better. New skiers learn faster, experienced skiers tackle more difficult terrain and snow conditions, and people ski at higher levels later into their lives. As Warren Miller might say, shaped skis are the best thing to happen to the sport since stretch pants.

The new equipment has caused the ski teaching and coaching community to reconsider just about everything we thought we knew about how to ski and how to teach skiing. Most of what we thought we knew, we still think we know. But there are some things that I, for one, have either changed my mind about or have come to realize I didn't have quite right. I've been asked many times if I would write a second edition of *The Skier's Edge* that addresses these changes, and this book is, in part, that second edition. The core topics are still here, but the material has been revised and augmented to identify the changes brought by shaped skis and explain why they've occurred. There are six new chapters, four of which are in a new section on tactics and techniques for specific types of advanced skiing: ice, moguls, powder, and steeps. Not only has ski technology improved in the last 11 years, but so has photographic technology, and almost every photo in the book is new.

Although many new techniques of lasting value have emerged during the shaped ski revolution, none were invented by me or any other technical analyst. Rather, the best skiers retooled their skiing to take advantage of the new gear. What I've found is that, with few exceptions, the best skiers still make the same movements they always have. This shouldn't be surprising. After all, neither the laws of physics nor the structure of the human body has changed—only our skis. What have changed in ski technique, in many cases, are the relative amplitudes of some movements, how often they're made, and their timing relative to each other and the phases of the turn. These changes, and how the new skis have brought them about, are discussed in detail in this book.

I believe that most changes in ski technique aren't deliberately invented by anyone. I think they evolve in a Darwinian fashion, emerging from the feet of talented skiers all over the world in response to changes in the skiing environment. What works survives. And what changes in the skiing environment is, for the most part, our equipment.

In the preface to *The Skier's Edge,* I wrote that Vic Braden, the noted tennis coach, once told me that every great coach he had known understood the physics of his sport and of human movement. If you're an avid skier, you are, for the most part, your own coach. You improve by watching better skiers, talking with your friends, picking up tips here and there, and, maybe, reading books like this one. But chances are you don't have the understanding of the sport that Braden (and I) would think you need to be the best coach you can be, and therefore the best skier you can be.

This book will help you ski better by becoming that coach: the one who understands the sport well enough to analyze, evaluate, and modify what you are doing. This book explains how the skis, the snow, and you, the skier, work together to make skiing happen, including the basic mechanics of the sport, the movements you make to take advantage of and control these mechanics, and how you can apply them out on the mountain in the real world of skiing.

You don't need formal training in physics or kinesiology to be a good coach or a skier, and I don't intend to provide that. The mechanics of skiing are pretty simple and I hope to explain them in terms of everyday experience and what you feel when you ski. If I have done my job, you should, as you read, come to understand the more technical material by thinking, *So that's what I feel when I make a turn!* This touches on an issue at the heart of coaching and skiing. As coaches and instructors, we often confuse what we teach with how we teach it. And as skiers, we often confuse what we feel with what we actually do. My objective is to untangle that confusion so you know what is fact and what is feeling—so you know what the goal is and what you need to do to reach it.

Of course you need more than an academic understanding of skiing to coach yourself toward better performance. You need images, visual and visceral, that you can absorb and emulate when you're out on the slopes. With this in mind, I supply photographs and photomontages, picked for their ability to expose certain techniques and convey particular concepts, of some of the best skiers in the world, and descriptions of what you should feel when you pull off a specific movement. Many of the images show World Cup athletes in competition. These athletes are, in my opinion, the best skiers in the world, technically speaking. They don't get judged on style, only on how effectively they handle challenging situations. People who've skied on slopes that have been prepared for World Cup races know how formidable they are. The snow is like formica, many of the pitches are precipitous, and the courses are *fast*. Skiers who look pretty darned good on the double-diamonds back home are instantly transformed into hackers by these race hills. In short, there's no doubt that someone who can win on the World Cup must be doing it right. There are also many photos of expert skiers whose technique is exemplary and deserves emulation. Finally, I've included images of skiers exhibiting particular common problems. Many of the photos are relevant to more than one topic, or chapter, in the book, so I occasionally point you to photos in other parts of the book that are good examples of the topic at hand.

Once you understand how skiing and ski technique work and have read about how good technique is supposed to feel, you need to practice. By that I don't mean just going out and making turns. I mean directed, focused execution of specific movements so that your body, not just your brain, learns what to do and how it feels. To this end, I've included exercises, drills, and cues to help direct your training.

The book is organized in three parts. Part I, comprising chapters 1 through 3, explains the basic mechanics of skiing, including how skis do their job. These aren't complicated. Unless you have novocaine in your bloodstream, you already know the mechanics of skiing by how they feel. Skiing is a sport of big, tangible forces, and when skiing feels good, it's the effects of those forces on your body that you feel. Once you understand how what you feel corresponds to the mechanics of skiing, everything about the sport will make more sense.

Part II, chapters 4 through 10, details the movements we make to work with the forces of skiing—why we make them and how. This is *technique:* the collection of movements we make with our bodies to summon up the right forces, and to get these forces to act in the right place at the right time. Part II also includes a chapter on boots. Every movement you make to control your skis works through your boots, and they must set up right if you're going to ski your best. If 20 pages on boots (chapter 10) sounds like overkill, think again. They are the most personal and important part of your equipment, and you can only ski as well as your boots let you.

Part III, chapters 11 through 14, examines real-world skiing in specific types of terrain and snow that are the bread and butter of advanced and expert skiing: ice, moguls, powder, and steeps. In these environments, the tactics you choose are as important as (and largely determine) the techniques you employ. We'll take a good look at both.

I mentioned that one of the reasons I wrote this book is because of the changes that have occurred with the new generation of skis. Another reason is that, over the past 10 years, I have had the good fortune of working with and learning from a good many knowledgable, gifted, and generous people. They have given me opportunities to learn that I could have only dreamed of; they have shared their knowledge and wisdom and disagreed constructively with me when it's mattered. I want to pass on what I've learned.

Most of all, I wrote this book to help you enjoy skiing more by skiing better.

Acknowledgments

This book has been made immeasurably better by the help, encouragement, and support of many people.

I'm indebted to the many great ski technicians whose books have taught me so much over the years. I have especially been influenced by Georges Joubert, James Major, and Olle Larsson. Their approach to analyzing skiing and their groundbreaking photomontages have been a model and inspiration.

I want to thank all of the skiers who gave me so many hours of their time and talent to ski for the noncompetition photos in the book. Their ability to demonstrate good skiing has made the job of writing about it much easier.

Megan Harvey and Ron Kipp gave me great detailed feedback on many of the topics on techniques, and Kurt Fahrenbach was instrumental in ironing out a few key points. Thanks to Don Daigle for reminding me of something I said and adding something to it.

Ron Kipp, Rodger Kramm of the University of Colorado, and Patrick Naylor at the Boulder Center for Sports Medicine gave me valuable advice and answered many questions pertaining to the book's biomechanics material.

For their careful review and advice on the physical mechanics sections, my thanks go to Juris Vagners, Chris Brown, and especially John Howe, who spent hours with me on the phone talking about how skis function.

Noah Finkelstein and Noah Podolefsky were a great help, over many burgers and beers, in clarifying the presentation of the physical mechanics of skiing. I want to thank them and my other former colleagues in the physics education research community at the the University of Colorado, where I learned something about how people learn.

Greg Hoffman at Ski Boot Fitting in Vail, Colorado, and Denny Hanson of Apex Sports Group in Boulder helped refine the material on boots. Greg and I have had some great discussions about boot fitting over the last few years, from which I've learned much.

I am grateful to the Rossignol Ski Company, and Jason Newell in particular, for their generous support over the years.

Richard Rokos of the University of Colorado Ski Team deserves special thanks for being there at a moment's notice when I needed help with photo shoots.

Without the help and advice on publishing from my old friend Paul Fargis, I'm not sure I would have undertaken this project in the first place. And without the ongoing help and encouragement of Mandy Eastin-Allen and Laurel Plotzke, my editors at Human Kinetics, I'm not sure I would have persevered to its completion. More than anyone, though, I want to thank Rick Kahl, a great editor and a good friend, who always answered the phone when I had yet another question about skiing or writing.

For many years, Dee Byrne of the Vail Ski and Snowboard School has made me feel a welcome part of the family of Vail ski pros. Dee, along with her colleagues Carol Levine and Brian Blackstock, has provided me access to the staff of the ski and snowboard school, who, by listening to my presentations and then asking me hard questions and telling me what they know, have helped me understand skiing better and improve my ability to express myself.

It's hard to put into words the special place Carol Levine and Curt Chase have had in the development of this book. Whenever I've needed help understanding something or just wanted to talk skiing with someone who cares about it as much as I do, they've been there for a lift ride, a glass of scotch, or just a phone call.

Finally, I want to thank the dedicated staff and athletes of the U.S. Ski Team. I'm especially indebted to Jesse Hunt, Finn Gundersen, Andy Walshe, and Phil McNichol. All have taught me a great deal and given me the opportunity to watch and analyze the best skiers in the world, and thus made this book possible.

PART I

Fundamentals:
Skiing From the Snow Up

Years ago I read an article about a well-known race-car driver that changed the way I think about skiing. The driver said that everything he did behind the wheel was motivated and judged by its effect on the four patches of contact his tires made with the pavement.

Since then I've come to believe that every element of ski technique can ultimately be evaluated in terms of how it affects our interaction with the snow. If we want to turn or slow down, we need the snow to push on us in a particular way, which means manipulating our skis in ways that extract the force from the snow that provides that push and aligning our bodies to balance against it. Where our skis meet the snow is where the rubber meets the road, so to speak.

The gravitational pull of the earth and the push of the snow are what make skiing happen. Because of these forces, our skis are designed the way they are, and we move our bodies the way we do. Once you understand the forces, everything else about skiing makes more sense. That's what part I is about: the simple, basic forces of skiing, how modern skis are designed to work with these forces to shape and carve turns, and how we work with the forces to produce the incredible variety of turns that make skiing so much fun.

Skiing Mechanics

Skiing is a sensual sport. We love what we feel when we ski. We love what we feel when we see another skier make a great turn. And what is it that we feel? Forces. The same forces that Sir Isaac Newton definitively characterized with his three elegant laws of motion. The forces that govern the movements of the planets and the balls on a pool table are the same forces that make skis turn and that make skiing feel so good.

1. An object that's not moving won't move unless something else exerts a force on it, and an object that's moving will continue to move at the same speed, in the same direction, unless something else exerts a force on it. For example, in skiing, gravity makes you move by pulling you down the hill. When the hill flattens out, friction between the skis and the snow and the air pushing against your body slow you down.

2. The magnitude of the change in an object's motion caused by a force is proportional to the size of the force and is inversely proportional to the object's mass. The direction of the change in the object's motion is the direction in which the force acts on the object. For instance, a gust of wind affects you more than the same gust affects a skier heavier than you. If the wind blows straight up the hill, it slows you down.

3. Forces always occur in pairs. Whenever one object exerts a force on a second object, the second object exerts a force of the same size on the first object, in exactly the opposite direction. When you pole across a flat on skis, you exert a force on the snow with your poles. The snow reacts by pushing back on you, providing the force that makes you move forward.

The basic mechanics of skiing aren't merely abstract concepts; they are the concrete forces that make skiing happen, and you feel them when you ski. In this chapter we discuss these basic physical mechanics because understanding them helps your skiing in a couple of ways. The techniques of the sport, covered in part II, have their basis in these physical mechanics, so fully understanding the techniques requires some understanding of the mechanics. Furthermore, the vocabulary of physical mechanics gives us the clearest, most objective way to talk about skiing with each other.

Forces, Pressure, and Momentum

In his famous *Lectures on Physics,* the late Nobel laureate and legendary physics professor Richard Feynman said, "Newton's laws . . . say pay attention to the forces. If an object is [changing speed or direction], some agency is at work; find it" (vol. I, ch. 9, p. 3). Skiing is all about changing speed and direction, which means changing momentum. So if we want to understand the mechanics of skiing, to follow Feynman's suggestion, we need to search for and understand the forces affecting the skier's momentum.

To start, we divide the forces in skiing into two categories: internal and external forces. Internal forces are those that skiers generate with their muscles. They're used to align segments of the body, manipulate the skis and poles, and push against the snow to get a desired reaction from it. Edging the ski by twisting the leg inward is an example of using an internal force to manipulate the ski. Turning the upper body down the hill at the end of a turn is an alignment movement created by internal forces. A quick extension to unweight the skis uses internal forces to push the skis downward against the snow. In contrast, external forces act on the skier from outside the body. Gravity, friction between the skis and snow, and wind resistance are some (but not all) of the external forces that can change a skier's motion. Gravity, the primal external force of interaction between your body and the earth, gives you momentum. Then, using your skis, you impress your momentum on the snow to evoke forces that make you turn or slow down.

Sometimes it's easier to think in terms of the pressure between your skis and the snow, rather than the force, so you'll see the term *pressure* occasionally in this book. Simply put, pressure is force spread over an area. When you're standing on skis in deep powder, you apply no less force to the snow than when you're standing in that snow without skis. But because you exert less force on each square inch of snow, you don't sink as far as when you're on foot. In contrast, if a person weighing twice as much as you comes along on a pair of skis the same size, that person will sink farther into the snow because twice as much pressure is being put on the snow. Controlling pressure and controlling force, then, often amount to the same thing for skiers.

Momentum is one of those cosmic fundamental properties of the universe that's a little hard to define. Isaac Newton called it a "quantity of motion"—the product of an object's mass and its velocity. The concept of momentum is more easily understood by observing its effects. Momentum is that property of a moving object that makes the object resist slowing down or changing direction. It's the property your car has when you're driving that keeps the car moving at the same speed until you hit the brakes or wind resistance and friction slow it down, and keeps it going in a straight line until you turn the wheel. Once you're moving on skis, you have momentum. Your momentum keeps you going at the same speed and in the same direction until an external force pushes on you. That last sentence is very important. You, the skier, only change direction or speed when an outside force acts on you. This is, essentially, Newton's first law of motion. (Exactly how your momentum changes when you're acted on by outside forces is the subject of Newton's second law, $F = ma$, where F is the sum of all outside forces, m is your mass, and a is your resulting acceleration.)

Forces and momentum have two key attributes: magnitude and direction. Gravity, for example, acts toward the center of earth. A T-bar exerts a force on you in the direction of its attachment to the cable. Throughout this book, we'll use arrows to represent forces and momentum. An arrow's length will correspond to the relative

Hermann Maier

In the late 1990s, Hermann Maier of Austria single-handedly raised the level of competition on the men's circuit with a combination of technical skill, physical power, and aggressive line.

Interestingly, his career has in many ways been defined not by his 54 victories (second only to Ingemar Stenmark on the men's side of the World Cup), his 14 overall and individual-discipline World Cup titles, and his numerous Olympic and World Championship medals, but by two crashes. The first was a spectacular fall he took in a downhill

training run at the 1998 Nagano Olympics. Photographer Carl Yarbrough caught Maier flying directly at him through the air, nearly upside down with nothing but blue sky behind him, grimacing in anticipation of what was sure to be a very painful landing. A lead picture in *Sports Illustrated* the next week, Yarbrough's shot made Maier an instant worldwide sports celebrity. Maier's response to this terrible crash? He won the Olympic super G and giant slalom races that week.

It was another crash, this one off the slopes, that has defined Maier's career in more fundamental ways. He was struck by a car in August 2001 while riding a motorcycle. The injuries to his right leg were so severe that doctors seriously considered amputating it, but instead performed extensive reconstructive surgery. This time, *Sports Illustrated* led with a two-page spread of Maier's X-rays. Many gave him little chance of ever skiing again, let alone competing at the highest level.

Maier responded to the smashed leg with a year and a half of relentless rehab. Not only did he return to World Cup competition, but he also amazed everyone by winning the second race he entered—the super G at Kitzbühel, Austria, one of the most demanding hills in the world. The next season he stunned the skiing world again by winning his fourth overall World Cup and fifth super G crown. All this on a right leg he claimed was so numb that he couldn't feel the front of his boot. Although Hermann Maier is probably nearing the end of his career, he continues to be successful, particularly in super G. When he does retire, he will leave a legacy not only as an excellent skier, but as a person who rises above adversity.

magnitude of the force or momentum, and the arrow's direction will correspond to the direction in which the force or momentum acts. The force of gravity acting on something can be represented by an arrow pointing toward the center of the earth. If one thing weighs twice as much as another, the magnitude of the gravitational force on it will be twice as big, and so the arrow would be twice as long. A skier's momentum can be shown by an arrow pointing in the direction the skier is traveling, its length proportional to the skier's speed and weight. If two skiers of the same weight are going at different speeds, the magnitudes of their momentums will be different, and so the arrows representing them will be of different lengths. Similarly, the momentums of skiers of different weights going the same speed will have different magnitudes. The exact lengths of the arrows we use aren't important, as long as the relative lengths of the arrows used in the same picture reflect the relative magnitudes of the forces and momentums they represent.

Slowing down corresponds to a decrease in the magnitude of your momentum. This happens only if you meet with a force acting at least partially in opposition to your direction of travel. You turn when your momentum's direction changes, not its magnitude, and this happens only if a force pushes on you from the side. Figure 1.1 shows how these effects can be isolated or can happen at the same time, depending on the direction in which an external force acts on you.

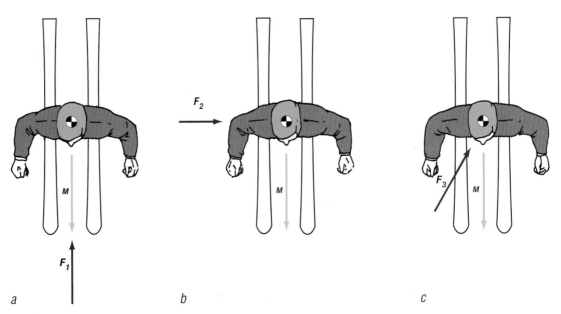

FIGURE 1.1   *(a)* The force, F_1, reduces the magnitude of the skier's momentum, M, because F_1 directly opposes it. *(b)* F_2, because it acts perpendicular to M, changes the direction of the skier's momentum, but not its magnitude. *(c)* F_3 both slows and turns the skier because it acts from both the front and the side.

The Skier's Center of Gravity

As we've seen, your direction and the speed at which you're going changes only when an outside force acts on you. So, at the most fundamental level, ski technique is about managing forces, particularly gravity and the force from the snow, which we'll explore shortly. To understand how to manage these forces, we first need to understand how they affect a skier's motion, and for that we rely on the concept of the skier's center of gravity.

If we were to try to determine the overall effect of a force on a skier by considering its specific effect on each of the skier's body segments, we would be faced with a difficult job. But we can get the same result more easily by considering the effect of the force on a single point: the skier's center of gravity. Also, as we'll see later in this chapter and throughout the book, a skier's balance is best understood in terms of the center of gravity. For these reasons, the center of gravity is an indispensable concept for understanding the mechanics of skiing. (It is, for all practical purposes, identical to the center of gravity.)

A body's center of gravity is the point about which all its weight is evenly balanced. If you toss an object spinning into the air, it spins about its center of gravity. For a simple, rigid, symmetrical object like a basketball, the center of gravity might lie at the object's geometric center. The center of gravity of an irregularly shaped rigid object, like a boomerang, might lie outside the object itself (figure 1.2).

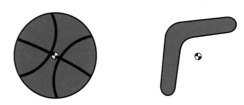

FIGURE 1.2   An object's center of gravity can lie inside or outside the object.

Things get a bit more complicated for objects that have movable segments, such as the human body, because the location of such an object's center of gravity can change as the segments move in relation to each other. A person's center of gravity isn't a fixed point. For a person standing erect with arms hanging at each side, the center of gravity lies approximately in line with the navel a few centimeters in front of the spine. But the location of the center of gravity changes as the person flexes, extends, twists, and turns, and often lies outside the body. Figure 1.3 shows the approximate location of the center of gravity for a skier in some common skiing positions.

FIGURE 1.3   The location of a skier's center of gravity in some common skiing postures. Skier: Jerry Berg.

Each body segment has its own center of gravity, too, and in some circumstances each must be considered independently. If, for example, the skier relaxes the muscles of the lower back and thighs when skiing into a bump, the centers of gravity of the upper and lower legs, boots, and skis will be pushed upward by the bump. Those of the body segments above the hips, though, will actually be pulled downward by gravity (figure 1.4).

FIGURE 1.4   As this skier flexes and extends across the mogul, her upper body's center of gravity travels a different path than that of her lower legs, boots, and skis. Skier: Cait Boyd.

Force From the Snow

Once gravity has given us momentum, most everything we accomplish on skis depends on how the snow interacts with us. We want to go fast, and the snow obliges by being slippery. We want to slow down, and the snow dutifully pushes on us, resisting our momentum. We want to turn, and the snow pushes us in the direction we want to go.

FIGURE 1.5 The force of the snow pushing against the bottom of the ski makes the skier turn. Skier: Hermann Maier, Austria.

The snow pushes on you in two ways. First, there's friction between the snow and the bottoms of your skis. This is one of the two main forces that slows you down when you're going in a straight line with your skis pointed straight ahead. (The other force is wind resistance.) Friction can only slow you down: It can't make you turn. It acts in a direction parallel to the bases of your skis, it's more or less constant, and there's little you can do to change it other than tune and wax your skis.

The other force from the snow, the one that really makes skiing interesting, is its resistance to being compressed and broken up. It's this quality of snow that provides the force—pushing on you perpendicular to the bottoms of your skis—that makes you turn or slow down (figures 1.5 and 1.6). It's the force from the snow that propels you through one curving arc to another. It's the force from the snow that addicts you to the sport.

FIGURE 1.6 The snow's resistance to being packed and broken up slows the skier down. Skier: Cait Boyd.

Packing a handful of snow into a snowball takes force and energy. The harder it's packed, the more the snow resists, and the more force it takes to pack it tighter. You push against it, and it pushes back. When you push against the snow with your skis you exert an *applied force* on the snow. The snow reacts by pushing back on you with a *reaction force.* When you're standing still, the snow is simply reacting to your weight. When you're moving and put the ski at an angle to your motion, the snow reacts to your momentum (your mass and velocity) by exerting a more interesting reaction force on you: one that can make you turn or slow you down. It's this reaction force that controls your speed and direction. The rest of this book is about that force—how we adjust its magnitude and its direction so that we go where we want to go at the speed we choose.

Different types of snow react differently to your applied force. Skiing on hard snow is like making a snowball with wet, slushy snow. You don't have to compress it much before it pushes back so hard that you can't pack it tighter. Skiing in powder is like making a snowball with dry, light snow. You have to do a lot of compacting before the snow holds together and offers you some resistance (figure 1.7). Ice or very hard snow may show virtually no compression and needs to be cut by the ski's edge to provide a surface that can hold the skier.

Because the ski's base is so slippery, the snow's reaction force is always perpendicular to it. This is an important fact that tells us a lot about how we need to position our bodies relative to our feet to be in balance and to get the effect we want from the snow. Consider what it means for you to have your center of gravity "over your feet." It means that a line drawn through your center of gravity perpendicular to the bottoms of your skis passes through your feet, as shown in figure 1.8. That line matches the direction the snow pushes on you, not the direction gravity pulls on you. So, as you go through turns, over bumps, and through dips, the force coming from the snow will always be pushing upward through the skis, perpendicular to their bases. This is the force you must balance against.

FIGURE 1.7 Powder snow must be packed until it can push back hard enough on the skier to make him turn or slow down. Skier: Charley Stocker.

FIGURE 1.8 Throughout the book, we'll use *R* to label the force the skier exerts, coming from the center of gravity, on the snow, and *S* for the force the snow exerts on the skier. In the most fundamental and important sense, this skier's center of gravity is over his feet. Skier: Bob Barnes.

FIGURE 1.9 A well-balanced pack increases the skier's mass without affecting his center of gravity much fore and aft or laterally. The pack increases the effects of the skier's movements on both the skis' behavior and the load on the skier's muscles, making it a simple and effective training tool. Skier: Ron LeMaster.

Photo courtesy of Bob Barnes

To become more sensitive to the force from the snow and how to balance against it, try amplifying the force by skiing with a loaded pack, as shown in figure 1.9. By increasing your mass, the pack increases your momentum and the force you apply to the snow, and hence the snow's reaction force. A few hours of skiing with a pack that increases your weight by 10 or 15 percent will quickly improve your sensitivity to the forces of skiing, your balance, and technique.

Accomplished skiers use the force from the snow as their gyroscope. They feel for it, balance against it, and judge the quality of their skiing by it. When you've learned to feel for and balance against this force, you've learned a fundamental lesson of skiing—that how it *feels* is the most important measure of its quality.

Centrifugal Force

To understand how we balance while turning and how that relates to what we feel when we're doing it, it's helpful to use the concept of *centrifugal force,* an important mechanical element in the skier's frame of reference (explained at the end of this chapter).

Every one of us has a personal, subjective understanding of centrifugal force. We feel its effects every time we make a turn on skis, on a bicycle, or in a car. It's the force that wants to fling us to the outside of the turn. What we feel, in actuality, is the snow, the pavement, or the seat of the car pushing on us, resisting our momentum and propelling us in a curve. If you strapped an accelerometer (a standard force-measuring instrument) on your back, it would measure the centrifugal force that you feel.

Centrifugal force isn't a true force in the strictest sense. Rather, it's an *apparent force:* something you feel to be a force when you're in a turn. It's the result of other external forces that are pushing you in a curved path, principally the force from the snow we talked about earlier. (The external motive force from the snow that makes the skier turn is a *centripetal force,* meaning it's directed toward the center of the turn. The centrifugal force the skier experiences is caused by the centripetal force from the snow.)

To someone who's standing still and watching you ski, centrifugal force doesn't exist. But to you, it's completely real—so much so that by adopting your frame of reference, we can make meaningful and accurate analyses of your skiing. And because you're the one doing the skiing and the one thinking about ski technique, centrifugal force is not only a valid concept for describing skiing, but completely appropriate.

Centrifugal force acts in a direction straight outward from the center of the turn, and its magnitude is a function of the radius of the turn, your speed, and your weight (figure 1.10). Cut the radius of the turn in half, and the centrifugal force doubles (because it's inversely proportional to the radius). Double your speed, and the centrifugal force quadruples (because it's proportional to the square of the speed). This has significant implications for lateral balance and turn radius, which we'll see later in this chapter and in chapter 2, when we address carving.

FIGURE 1.10   These two cyclists are going at the same speed, but the one in white is making a tighter turn. As a result, he experiences a bigger centrifugal force and must incline more into the turn. The same is true for skiers: To make a tighter turn at a given speed, you must incline farther into the turn.

The Resultant Force on the Skier: Gravity and Centrifugal Force Combined

From the skier's point of view, the three biggest forces at work in a turn are gravity, centrifugal force, and the force from the snow, which is its reaction to the combined effect of the first two.

When two or more forces—in this case gravity and centrifugal force—act on a body, they have an additive effect, as if the body were being acted on by a single force. Put another way, we could replace those forces with a single force equal to their sum, and the body would react in exactly the same way. That single force, their combined effect on you, is called the *resultant* of the other forces. It's something we'll talk about over and over in this book.

FIGURE 1.11 Centrifugal force, *C*, combines with the force of gravity acting on the skier's mass, *G*, to form the resultant force *R* acting on the skier. *S* is the reaction force produced by the snow in response to *R*. Skier: Annie Black.

To be in balance in a turn, your inclination must match the inclination of the resultant of gravity acting on your mass, and centrifugal force, as shown in figure 1.11. The resultant passes through your base of support, and the reaction force from the snow, is exactly equal in magnitude and opposite in direction to that resultant.

It's easy to find the resultant of two forces. We simply draw an arrow for each force, with their tails anchored to the center of gravity, then draw a box (strictly speaking, a parallelogram) using those arrows as sides. A new arrow marking the diagonal of the box is the resultant. If we need to, we can add a third force now by combining it in the same manner with the resultant of the first two, thereby finding the resultant of all three forces. Any number of forces can be added together in this way.

Based on the skier's inclination, we can determine how much force is experienced in a turn. Results for some typical inclinations, expressed in Gs (multiples of the skier's weight), are shown in the following list. A good advanced recreational skier can make turns at about 20 degrees of inclination, and might occasionally reach 30 degrees. Technically strong experts do a lot of their skiing at 30 to 45 degrees. World-class racers have been making giant slalom turns at 60 degrees since around the year 2000, and have recently been making turns at angles as high as 70 degrees. Turns made at inclinations greater than 45 degrees require exceptional physical and technical strength to balance against the large forces involved.

Inclination	*Force*
0 degrees	1G
20 degrees	1.1G
30 degrees	1.2G
45 degrees	1.4G
60 degrees	2G
70 degrees	2.9G

We can also break forces down into separate *components*. If the wind is blowing at you from the northwest, you could say that part of its force is coming from the north and part from the west. These would be components of the wind's force. If the wind shifted to come more from the north, we'd say that its northern component had gotten stronger, and its western component weaker.

We'll often need to find components of some force in skiing to get a more detailed understanding of how that force affects the skier. Most often it will be some force of interaction between the ski and the snow, and the components will tell us something about how the ski holds or slips, or how the skier turns or slows down.

To resolve a force into two components we essentially reverse the process of finding a resultant. We draw a box with that force as its diagonal. The sides of the box attached to the force's tip are then two components that could make up that force. Figure 1.12 shows some ways of resolving the reaction force from the snow.

a   *b*

FIGURE 1.12 *(a)* The reaction force from the snow, *S*, is resolved into a component that opposes gravity, S_p, and keeps the skier from sinking into the snow, and one that pushes on her laterally, S_l, parallel to the snow's surface, in direct opposition to the centrifugal force. *(b)* S_l can further be broken into a component that slows the skier down, S_d, and one that makes him turn, S_t. Their angles to the skier's momentum, *M,* not his ski, determine their effect on his motion. Skiers: *(a)* Annie Black; *(b)* Jerry Berg.

We could draw any number of different boxes for which the original force serves as a diagonal, and indeed any number of component pairs could be drawn for that original force. The pair we choose is determined by what we want to find out. In the case of figure 1.12*b*, for instance, we're interested in how much of the force from the snow is making the skier turn, and how much is slowing him down.

Twisting Actions

The forces and momentum we have talked about so far all act in straight lines. They are *linear.* There is another class of force and momentum related to twisting actions. A twisting force is a *torque* (pronounced 'tórk). and the momentum that a spinning body has is called *angular momentum.* You crank a corkscrew into a wine bottle by applying a torque to it. When you turn a bolt with a wrench, the handle acts as a lever arm, and the force you apply to the handle puts a torque on the bolt. The longer the handle, the longer the lever arm through which the force works, and the greater the torque. As we'll see later in chapters 7 and 8, torques play important roles in turning the skis and holding them on edge.

Just as your linear momentum will only change if an external force acts on you, you will have no angular momentum unless an external torque acts on you. For this reason, your entire body will rotate in the air only if a torque acts on it before it leaves the ground. The skier in figure 1.13 does this by throwing his upper body around just before he leaves the takeoff. The snowboarder in figure 1.14 leaves the ground with no angular momentum, so he has no net rotation in the air.

A body that's spinning has angular momentum. A top spinning in one place has no linear momentum but has plenty of angular momentum. When you throw a Frisbee you give it both linear and angular momentum.

Angular momentum is related to how fast the body is spinning and what we might call its swing weight, or its *moment of inertia.* A body's swing weight is related to

FIGURE 1.13   This skier gives himself angular momentum before he leaves the takeoff by rotating his upper body while his skis are still on the snow. As a result, he continues to rotate until he lands.

FIGURE 1.14   This snowboarder leaves the takeoff with no angular momentum. Once he's in the air he swings his arms in one direction and turns the board in the other, then straightens them out before he lands. The physical mechanism involved is similar to counterrotation, discussed in chapter 7. Note that the snowboarder could not complete a smooth, continuous 360-degree rotation, as the skier in figure 1.13 does, because he had no angular momentum when he left the takeoff.

how its mass is distributed relative to the axis about which it's turning. A ski has a much smaller swing weight, for instance, about a longitudinal axis (the axis it rotates around when you edge it) than it does about a vertical axis (the one it turns around when you pivot it into a turn). And a short, fat ski will have a smaller swing weight about a vertical axis than a long, skinny ski of the same weight.

The greater an object's swing weight, the more torque is required to give it a certain amount of angular momentum. That's why short skis are easier to pivot into a turn than long ones. In contrast, the weight of your boots and bindings doesn't have as big an effect on pivoting because they are closer to the rotational axis.

Balance and Toppling

A body is in static balance and won't fall over as long as the resultant of all forces acting on its center of gravity passes through the body's base of support (figure 1.15). It's in dynamic balance if, in addition, there are no unbalanced torques on the body that will make it spin (or change the rate that it's spinning if it already is).

If the force on a body passes outside its base of support, the body will be out of balance and topple, as we see the skier doing in figure 1.16. That might sound like a bad thing for a skier, but as we'll see in chapter 9, the ability to deliberately topple and recover with precision is an essential skill that sets expert skiers apart from the rest. If you ski in a wide stance, you are like a box with a big base: The stance provides a stable base of support and, barring sharp, unforeseen jolts, you're stable as you move along. If you were to stop moving, nothing in your stance would need to change to prevent you from falling over. On the other hand, an expert in a typical narrow stance, about hip width, is more like a broomstick you balance on your outstretched hand. Most of an expert's weight is usually balanced over the outside ski, and the skier is seldom in perfect, static balance. Rather, the expert is constantly making small adjustments in response to changes in force from the snow, just as you must constantly move your hand to keep the broomstick from falling over. And

FIGURE 1.15 This snowboarder is in balance because gravity, the force acting on him through his center of gravity, goes through the rail he's grinding: his base of support.

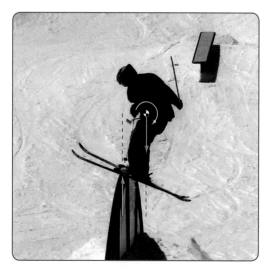

FIGURE 1.16 This skier is toppling off the rail because the force acting on him through his center of gravity falls outside his base of support. Note that because the forces don't line up with each other, they impart a torque on the skier.

as we'll see later, in chapter 9, linking high-performance parallel turns requires the skier to literally fall from one turn into the next.

It's understandable that people should be uncomfortable with the idea of being out of balance. But it is precisely that period of controlled falling from one turn into the next that gives us the floating, flying sensations that keep us coming back for more. The intermediate skier in a wide, stable stance has the stability of a child on a tricycle, but the seasoned skier flowing from turn to turn feels the deepest thrills of the sport.

The Skier's Frame of Reference

You might think that the proper description and analysis of the forces of skiing are universal—that they should be the same for someone skiing down the hill as they are for someone on the side of the hill watching the first one go by. It isn't so. Take the concept of centrifugal force. To the stationary observer, there's no such thing as centrifugal force acting on the moving skier. A complete and accurate analysis of the moving skier's motion doesn't include such a force. But for a skier making a turn, centrifugal force is entirely real, meaningful, and measurable. The difference is that the two people have different *frames of reference:* One is moving along a curved path, and the other is not. We will consistently choose to view the world through the eyes of the skier in motion because that reflects our personal understanding of the sport. We understand it from how it feels while we're making turns down the hill, not from how it looks when we see someone else doing it.

Biomechanical descriptions of human motion are generally based on a formally defined frame of reference, and ours will be too. For that definition we'll use the planes of the body defined by conventional biomechanics and physiology, as shown in figure 1.17, and anchor them on an axis specially chosen for describing skiing.

The axis that anchors our framework is a line through the skier's center of gravity that's aligned with the resultant of gravity and centrifugal force acting on the skier. You might notice that when the skier is in balance, this line is the same as the line of action of the force from the snow. We'll call it simply the *balance axis,* and we'll refer to it throughout the book. As previously mentioned, this axis goes through the skier's center of gravity, somewhere in front of the navel, and it's constantly tilting one way or another as the skier goes in and out of the fall line and through turns (figure 1.18). About the only time the balance axis is aligned with gravity is when the skier is in a straight run on a perfectly flat surface or in a perfectly flat traverse.

The planes we use are the *frontal, transverse,* and *sagittal* planes. Again, see figure 1.17. The sagittal plane divides the skier into left and right parts and goes through the balance axis. The frontal plane divides the body into front and back halves and also goes through the balance axis. Finally, the transverse plane divides the skier's body into upper and lower parts and is perpendicular to the balance axis.

You can easily feel the balance axis when you're skiing. It's the line along which all the pressure on your body and skis is focused when you're arcing a turn, setting your edges on a steep slope, or skiing into a mogul. Even when you're not skiing, you can feel it. Stand and rock from one foot to the other, and from your heel to your toe. The spot where you feel the maximum pressure on the soles of your feet tells you where the balance axis is fore and aft in the sagittal plane. If the pressure is equal on both your feet, the balance axis is right between them in the frontal plane.

As these terms and concepts come up in the following chapters, don't hesitate to come back here to refresh your understanding of them. The more comfortable you are with them, the better you'll understand the material in the book and the sport itself.

FIGURE 1.17   The standard planes of reference. Skier: David N. Oliver.

FIGURE 1.18   When a skier is in a turn, the balance axis and the entire frame of reference tilts toward the inside of the turn. Skier: Hermann Maier, Austria.

Skis, Snow, and Motion Control

Our skis are the instruments we use to extract and manage force from the snow. By manipulating our skis properly, through our boots, we get the snow to push on us with just the right amount of force and in just the right direction to control our speed and direction. Comprehending these interactions and how they produce the turns we make provides the basis for understanding the skidding, carving, and everything in between we do when we make turns on skis; this understanding is essential if we are to appreciate the techniques we use to produce those actions. In this chapter we discuss how skis and snow interact and how those interactions control our motion.

The Ski's Three Control Angles

Your motion down the hill is controlled by the interaction forces between your skis and the snow. These forces are controlled by three angles.

- The ski's *platform angle*—the angle between the force you apply to the ski and the platform the ski cuts in the snow—determines whether the ski holds or slips.
- The ski's *steering angle*—the angle between your direction of travel and the direction in which the ski is pointed—determines how much the ski–snow interaction force slows you down, and how much it makes you turn.
- The ski's *edge angle*—the angle between the bottom of the ski and the surface of the snow—determines how much the ski bends in a turn, thus affecting the radius of the turn.

These three angles are the principal controls we have over our skis and how they define our path down the hill. Most of ski technique boils down to managing these angles and then balancing against the skis.

The Ski's Platform Angle

Why does a ski slip? What makes it hold? From their first day on the snow, all skiers grapple with these questions. When we say we want the ski to hold, we're really saying that we want the snow to exert enough force on us to prevent any sideways movement. Our intuition tells us that the more we edge the ski, the better it will hold—that a more radically edged ski is like a sharper knife. That's only half true. The physical mechanics that determine whether a ski holds or slips aren't complicated, but they're not obvious, either. They boil down to two things: The ski has to penetrate the snow, cutting a platform in it that will support you, and the angle between that platform and the force you apply to it, the *platform angle,* must be 90 degrees or smaller. If the angle is greater than 90 degrees, the platform will slope away from you, and the ski will slip.

Many skiers share the misconception that the angle between the edge of the ski and the snow surface determines how well the ski holds. This isn't the case. Rather, it's the angle between the bottom of the ski and the force the skier applies that determines whether it will hold or not.

We all know that it's harder to put on a ski when you're standing on a slope than when you're on a flat. That's because the ski is slippery, and the snow can only push perpendicular to its base (figure 2.1). When you're on a slope, that force isn't lined up exactly opposite to gravity, which is the other force acting on the ski. The unbalanced component of gravity pushes the ski sideways toward the bottom of the hill.

What do you do to make your ski easier to put on when you're on a slope? You jam it into the snow to make a level step on which it can rest while you finagle your boot into the binding. The level step helps because now when the snow pushes perpendicular to the bottom of your ski, it's pushing in the exact opposite direction of gravity, and thus completely opposes it. The key is that the surface against which your skis are pushing is perpendicular to the force acting on it, the force of your weight.

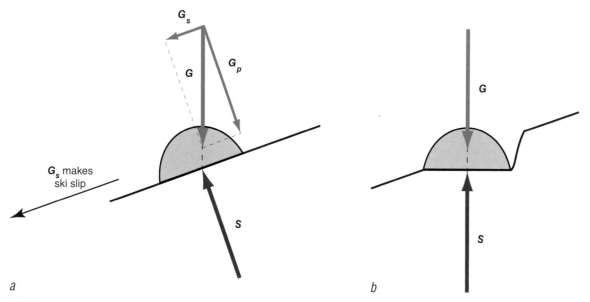

FIGURE 2.1   What makes a ski slip, and what makes it hold? Both skis in this figure, which are placed sideways on a slope, are acted on only by gravity, *G,* and a reaction force from the snow, *S.* Because the ski is slippery, *S* can only act perpendicularly to the ski's base. For the ski on the left, *S* can only oppose G_p, the component of G that is also perpendicular to the ski's base. This leaves an unbalanced component of gravity, G_s, that makes the ski slip. The ski on the right feels no unbalanced forces and does not slip.

FIGURE 2.2 The skier stands on a platform that the ski cuts in the snow. The angle of that platform to the force she exerts on it, the platform angle, determines whether the ski slips or holds. Skier: Annie Black.

You're faced with a similar task when trying to make your ski hold in a traverse. Again, you want the bottom of your ski to cut a step in the snow that's perpendicular to the force you're applying to the ski, or else you'll slip.

Things change a bit, but not that much, when you're in a turn. Now you apply the combined effect of gravity and centrifugal force to the ski. The force you apply to the ski is no longer directed toward the center of the earth but rather at an inclined angle. To keep from slipping, you and the ski need to be supported by a step that's perpendicular to this resultant force. In both the traverse and the turn, it's not the angle of the ski's edge to the snow that determines whether it slips or holds, it's the angle of the ski's edge to the force you apply to it: the platform angle (figure 2.2).

Consider the two skis shown in figure 2.3. R is the force the skier applies to the ski, S is the reaction force from the snow. The base of the ski on the left in figure 2.3 is perpendicular to R, meaning its platform angle is 90 degrees. It cuts a small step in the snow, and the snow responds with a reaction force exactly equal and opposite to the force applied to it by the skier. The ski holds. The base of the ski on the right in figure 2.3 is not perpendicular to the force R acting on it: Its platform angle is more than 90 degrees. It cuts a step in the snow that slopes away to the left from the force R, and so the ski will slip.

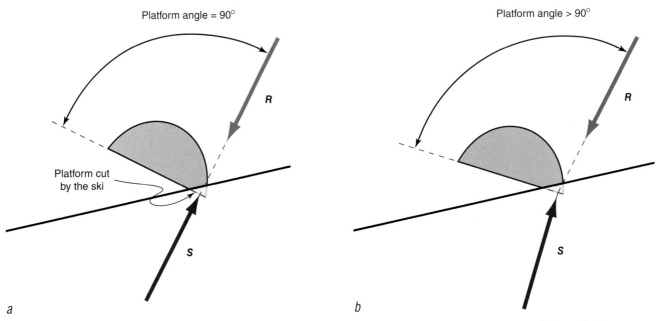

a   *b*

FIGURE 2.3 Making the ski hold in a turn is the same as in a traverse: It must cut a platform in the snow that's perpendicular to the force you apply to that platform. The ski on the left holds because its platform angle is 90 degrees. The ski on the right has a platform angle that's more than 90 degrees, so the surface it cuts into the snow slopes away from the force R, and the ski slips.

A platform angle that slopes away from you also reduces the depth to which the ski penetrates the snow. Think of spreading butter on bread with a knife. If you hold the knife at a flatter angle as you slide it, the knife's edge smears the butter across the bread. If you hold the knife at a sharper "platform angle," the knife digs into the bread. Similarly, if you want your ski to hold in a turn, you must hold it at a platform angle of 90 degrees or less. If you want it to slip, you have to flatten the ski to increase the platform angle. Techniques for controlling the platform angle are discussed in chapter 8. Certain aspects of boot setup are also relevant here and are presented in chapter 10.

Of course, if the ski is to extract any force from the snow, it must give the snow something to push against. That means the ski must penetrate the snow. If the snow is soft, that's easy. Getting the edge to penetrate very hard snow or ice isn't so easy. Think of cutting vegetables with a knife. To cut a tomato, you don't have to push very hard on the knife to get it to cut. In fact, you might have to be very gentle to avoid crushing the tomato. But to cut a fresh carrot, you have to lean on the knife.

When the snow is hard, your challenge is to get the edge to penetrate the surface as deeply as you can. The first key is to apply all the force available to as small an area as possible, maximizing the pressure on the snow. This is the primary advantage a sharp edge has over a dull one: It spreads the available force over a smaller area than a dull edge does.

Applying all the force you can to one ski is the other key to penetrating hard snow. World Cup racers, who know better than anyone how to ski on ultrahard snow, will tell you that when the going gets tough, they stand on their outside ski.

Part of the force you apply to the ski's edge tries to make it slip, and part of the force tries to drive the edge downward into the snow. Figure 2.4 shows these components, which we'll call the slipping force and the penetrating force. If the snow is very hard, the snow will support the slipping force without breaking up, as long as you can get enough penetrating force to get the edge down into the snow. Simply put, you maximize the penetrating force, relative to the slipping force, when you put all your weight on one ski.

If this explanation sounds complicated, think of it this way: If you're making a turn with half your weight on your inside ski and half on your outside ski, there will be more slipping force on the outside ski than on the inside ski. At the same time, there will be less penetrating force on the outside ski than on the inside ski. In other words, your skis don't share the slipping and penetrating loads equally; the ski with the greater slipping load, the outside ski, is at a distinct disadvantage, which makes it prone to slip. The more weight you can put on the outside ski, the better the situation gets, and the better you hold.

FIGURE 2.4   The force that the skier applies to the snow, *R*, can be resolved into two components: one that makes the edge penetrate the snow, R_p, and another that makes it slip, R_s. Skier: Annie Black.

The Ski's Steering Angle

The force of the snow pushing upward on the bottom of your ski can make you turn, slow you down, or both. The proportions are determined by the ski's angle to your direction of travel, its *steering angle*.

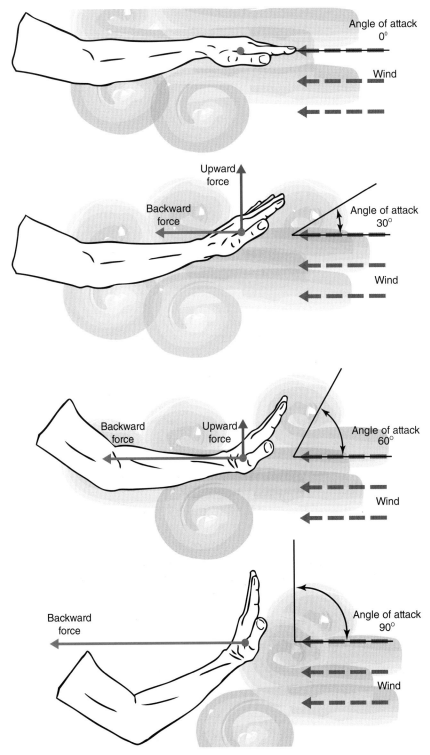

FIGURE 2.5 Forces on a "flying hand."

Imagine sticking your hand out the window of a moving car and flying it up and down through the wind. When the hand is flat, palm parallel to the pavement, it stays in one place. Given a little twist, the hand climbs or dives in the wind. Turned so the palm faces straight ahead (fingers pointed at the sky), the hand neither climbs nor dives but meets the maximum resistance to its forward motion (see figure 2.5).

Your hand applies a force to the air as it moves forward through it, and the air, resisting compression, pushes back with a reaction force. Regardless of how you hold your hand, the air is always exerting a force on it toward the rear of the car, trying to slow it. The backward force on the hand is smallest when the hand is perfectly level, and greatest when the hand is turned perpendicular to the wind. In neither of these positions is there any force pushing the hand up or down.

Between these two extremes, though, the air's reaction force has a vertical component. When the hand is at an angle to the wind (an aeronautical engineer would call this its *angle of attack*), there is another component of force: one that pushes the hand up or down. The graph in figure 2.6 shows, in approximate terms, how the upward component of the air's reaction force grows progressively as the angle of attack goes from 0 degrees to around 50 degrees. As the angle increases from that point, the upward force decreases.

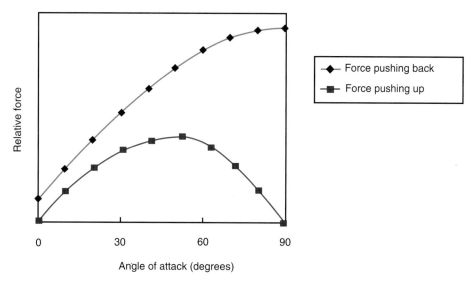

FIGURE 2.6   How forces on the flying hand change with the angle of attack.

The force finally dwindles to nothing when the angle of attack is 90 degrees. In comparison, the component of the air's reaction force pushing the hand back continues to grow steadily as the angle moves from 0 to 90 degrees.

The snow's reaction force pushes on the ski (and the skier) in much the same way as the air on your flying hand. What we called the hand's angle of attack, we call in skiing the steering angle. Before *you* can turn, your *ski* must turn, at least slightly (we'll talk about how slight the ski's turn can be when we discuss carving turns later in this chapter), which requires the ski to have a steering angle. It can attain that angle in three ways (also covered in detail later in this chapter): by being bent into reverse camber, by the steering angle provided by the ski's sidecut, or by the entire ski being pivoted. A ski running straight is like the hand out the window with palm parallel to the road. No force acts to change the ski's direction of travel. Pivoted 90 degrees to the skier's momentum, the ski elicits a reaction force from the snow that acts only to slow the skier. With the ski at any angle in between, the snow pushes on the skier like the wind on an angled hand. Some of the force acts to slow the skier, and some of it acts to change the direction of travel.

By varying the ski's steering angle, the skier alters the proportion of slowing and turning components of the snow's reaction force. A small steering angle results in a broad turn. A larger steering angle produces a sharper turn, but only up to a point. Beyond that point, increases in the steering angle cause more slowing but less turning. Many skiers do their skiing at steering angles of 45 degrees or more. Their skis work not so much to change their direction of travel as to keep their speed down by sliding sideways. They achieve their goal of speed control, but at the expense of one of skiing's great pleasures: the feeling of carving a round, clean, efficient turn, which generally requires smaller steering angles. Don't get me wrong: Expert skiers put their skis sideways in many situations—such as when making turns on very steep slopes or slowing down in confined spaces—but they separate the intention of slowing down from that of changing direction. This is an important distinction.

When we talk about steering angles, we're usually talking about a steering angle in the transverse plane—where the ski is pointed when you look down on it from above. The ski can also have a steering angle in the sagittal plane, which plays a significant role in carving turns, and is described later in this chapter. But unless I explicitly say a steering angle is in the sagittal plane, you should assume I mean a conventional steering angle in the transverse plane.

Your direction of travel changes when the middle of your ski is at an angle to your momentum. Look closely at the bottoms of your skis. I'll bet the biggest dings are right under the middle of the ski. The tip and tail probably look much better. Get your skis waxed and look at the bases after a half day of skiing. The wax will be worn off under the foot but probably not under the tip or tail. This is direct evidence that the big forces in skiing act directly under your feet. These are the forces that make you turn. The middle of the ski does the work of changing your direction of travel, largely as a result of the steering angle there. The tip and tail are simply not stiff enough to push very hard on you, and thus don't develop enough force to make you turn.

Compared to the force you apply to a ski—that is, your weight and centrifugal force—the ski is not very stiff. It typically takes only about 10 or 12 pounds to flatten one on the snow. From this point on, as you add more weight and centrifugal force, the pressure builds under the middle of the ski, but not much elsewhere. What this tells us is that the tip and tail of the ski do little to make you turn. What do they do, then? As you'll see in the next section, they make the ski itself turn.

The Ski's Edge Angle

Skis are subtle tools, with a spectrum of design points that make them do certain things very well. When a ski is rocked up on edge and pressured at an oblique angle to the surface of the snow, at an *edge angle* as shown in figure 2.7, certain key design features make it turn as it moves forward. I call this the ski's *self-steering effect*. All skiers use this effect to control their turns, whether they're carved or skidded. The design parameters that contribute most to the effect are the ski's *sidecut* and *longitudinal flex*, moderated by its *torsional flex*. When you see a skier make smooth, round turns with no noticeable pivoting of the skis, you're watching the skis' self-steering effect at work.

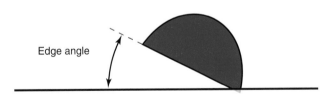

FIGURE 2.7 The ski's edge angle.

Sidecut

Viewed from above, skis have an hourglass shape, called *sidecut*. In almost all cases, the curve is circular. One of the important effects of sidecut is that when the ski is put on edge at a low to moderate angle to the snow, its steering angle varies along the ski's entire length. That steering angle is greatest at the shovel and decreases steadily toward the tail (figure 2.8a). Because the tip always has a greater steering angle than the rest of the ski, the ski will turn as it moves forward, even when it's skidding. The ski turns itself.

Interestingly, the sidecut doesn't have to be curved to have this effect (figure 2.8*b*). Assuming the ski is edged, the snow exerts a greater force against the edge of the forebody than against the tail because the forebody's steering angle is greater. The forebody and tail act like separate flying hands. They both draw reaction forces from the snow, but the direction each pushes is somewhat different. As a result, the ski turns as it moves forward.

Once the ski has turned itself, or the skier has turned it (discussed at length in chapter 7), the midbody of the ski will have a steering angle in the transverse plane that, in a manner similar to the "flying hand," will make the skier's path bend (figure 2.9*a*).

Longitudinal Flex and Reverse Camber

The ski's ability to flex from tip to tail, or *longitudinally*, is important in several ways: First, it allows the ski to run smoothly through bumps and irregularities in the snow surface without jarring the skier. Second, by spreading the force applied to the ski by the skier along its length, the ski's longitudinal stiffness helps the ski to run fast. Last but not least, it allows the ski to bend like a bow into *reverse camber* (an arc in which the middle of the ski is pushed outward relative to the tip and tail) when the skier tilts the

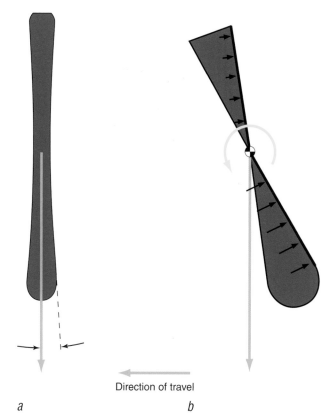

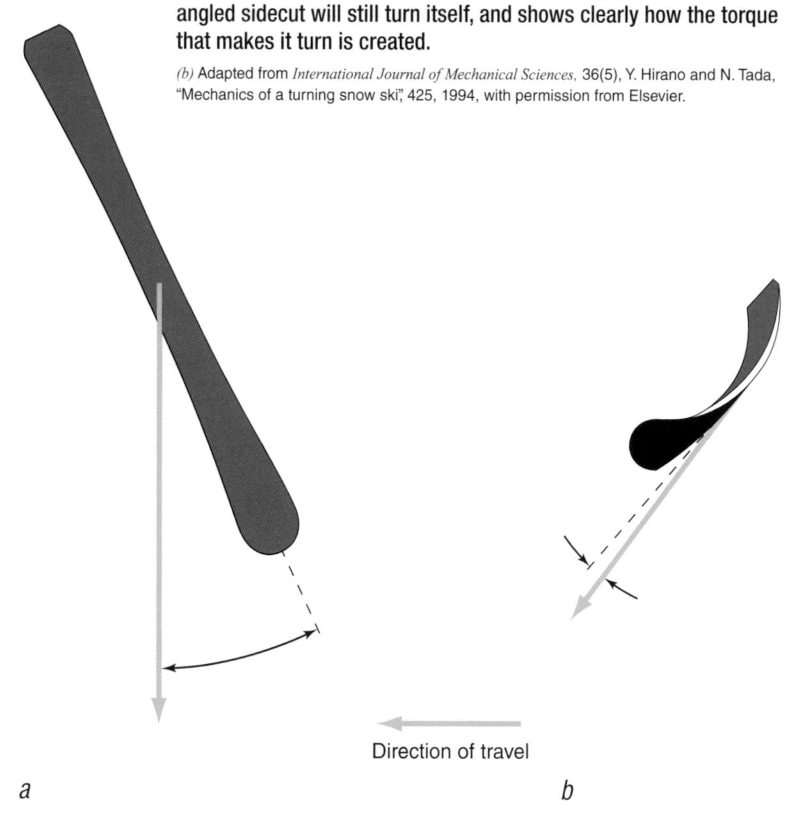

Direction of travel

a   *b*

FIGURE 2.8 Because of its sidecut, a ski's steering angle in the transverse plane varies along its length. As a result, if edged even slightly, it will turn itself as it moves forward. *(a)* A curved sidecut gives a ski its greatest steering angle at the tip. *(b)* This ski with an angled sidecut will still turn itself, and shows clearly how the torque that makes it turn is created.

(b) Adapted from *International Journal of Mechanical Sciences,* 36(5), Y. Hirano and N. Tada, "Mechanics of a turning snow ski", 425, 1994, with permission from Elsevier.

FIGURE 2.9 The ski can have steering angles in both the transverse and sagittal planes. *(a)* Turning the ski to the left or right relative to the direction of travel creates a steering angle in the transverse plane. This produces a force on the skier that will have both turning and slowing components. *(b)* When the ski bends into reverse camber, it creates a steering angle in the sagittal plane, resulting in a force that has very little slowing component. When a ski is carving (discussed later in this chapter), it is turning the skier through a steering angle in the sagittal plane. Note that the ski's reverse camber also makes the ski turn in the sagittal plane as it moves forward, and the deeper the reverse camber, the faster the ski will turn.

Direction of travel

a   *b*

FIGURE 2.10 Hermann Maier's left ski is bent into reverse camber as a function of its high edge angle to the snow, its sidecut, and the force applied to it. This causes a steering angle that varies along the ski's length, making both the ski and skier turn as it moves forward. The radius of the reverse camber, in an ideal situation, matches the radius of the turn. Notice in the third-to-last frame that the outside ski's forebody is bent more than the tail. This is caused by forward pressure on the ski. If Maier were to remain balanced this far forward throughout his turn, the ski would oversteer.

ski on edge and applies force to it (figure 2.10). This increases the relative difference between the tip and tail's steering angles in the sagittal plane (figure 2.9b). The more deeply the ski is bent into reverse camber, the greater the tip's relative steering angle, the smaller the tail's, and the greater the ski's self-steering effect.

When the ski is edged just slightly on firm or hard-packed snow, it scribes an arc that has the same radius as the ski's sidecut. As the ski is tilted to higher edge angles, it bends to keep the entire edge in contact with the snow, and the radius of the arc gets smaller. The higher the edge angle and the deeper the sidecut, the smaller the radius (figure 2.11a). A similar effect occurs on soft snow, but because the middle of the ski can penetrate the snow, the effect depends less on sidecut and more on the softness of the snow and the ski's flex (figure 2.11b).

If the platform angle is greater than 90 degrees, the ski won't hold perfectly but will still exhibit a self-steering effect and turn the skier. This, in combination with oversteering (see Skidding,

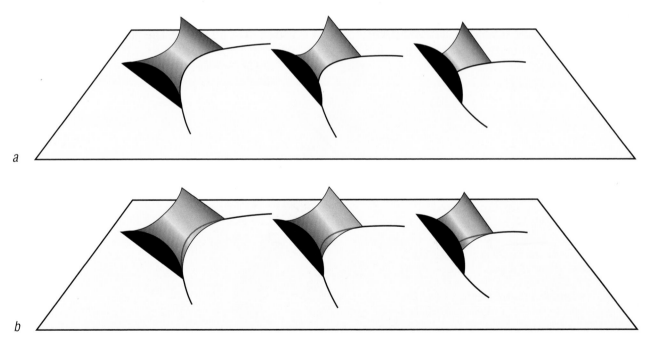

FIGURE 2.11 *(a)* Because of its sidecut, the ski cuts an arc of a smaller and smaller radius as its edge angle increases and it is bent into deeper reverse camber. *(b)* The ski in this figure has shallower sidecut than the ski in figure 2.11a. But because it's on soft snow and its midbody can penetrate the surface, the ski can cut the same radius arcs as those in figure 2.11a.

Oversteering, and Carving on p. 29), is how most skiers make turns. If the ski's platform angle is 90 degrees or less, it can hold and carve. Oversteering and carving are two important actions of the ski that we'll look at soon.

Pivoting the ski changes the steering angle of every point on the ski by the same amount. In contrast, edging and bending the ski increases the steering angle of the forebody more than the tail. By moving the distribution of pressure forward on the ski, the skier creates deeper bend in the forebody, accentuating the self-steering effect. By shifting pressure toward the tail, the skier reduces the load on the ski's forebody, reducing its bend and the self-steering effect.

Torsional Flex

There is one more physical characteristic of the ski that has an important bearing on the radius of arc the ski will describe on the snow: its *torsional flex*.

If you grab a garden hose in both hands and twist, the hose is flexing in torsion. This type of flexing is a key characteristic of each ski. In coordination with the ski's sidecut, torsion determines how aggressively the ski's extremities engage the snow when the ski is edged. The stiffer a ski is in torsion, the more it will bite at the tip and tail, and the greater will be its self-steering characteristics (all other things being equal). There are practical limits, however; a ski with a deep sidecut that's also very stiff in torsion will be edgy, difficult to pivot or make slip, and uncomfortable going from turn to turn for many skiers.

No ski is perfectly rigid in torsion. They all twist when loaded and edged. Because of this flex, the ski grips most in the middle and less and less aggressively toward its extremities. The platform angle of the ski on the left in figure 2.12 is 90 degrees under the skier's foot. The middle of the ski will hold well. But because the ski flexes in torsion, the tip and tail will have greater platform angles, won't grip as well, and will have a weaker turning effect on the ski. The ski on the right in figure 2.12 has been edged more so the platform angle at the tip is 90 degrees. Now the tip and tail will hold well, deepening the reverse camber and making the ski turn more sharply.

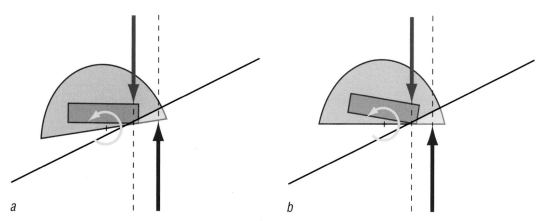

a   b

FIGURE 2.12 Because the ski flexes in torsion, its platform angle varies along its length. As the skier edges it more, the ski bites better further toward the tip and tail, increasing its self-steering effect.

Evolution of Ski Design

When all else is equal, a ski with a deeper sidecut exhibits more self-steering effect, as will a ski stiffer in torsion, because either condition gives the ski more bite at the tip and tail. If the ski is not too stiff longitudinally, it will bend easily and carve tight arcs. Making skis like this hasn't always been possible.

When skis were made of wood, longitudinal and torsional flex couldn't be controlled independently. They were either both stiff or both soft. And if a ski was soft enough to bend easily longitudinally, it also broke easily. Stein Eriksen was known for favoring such soft, limber boards—and also for breaking them.

Aluminum revolutionized skis in the 1950s by providing some independence in longitudinal and torsional stiffness. To this day, aluminum is used in race skis for its smoothness and rigidity in torsion, allowing for skis with aggressive—and unforgiving—grip. Fiberglass construction, especially when applied in torsion box designs first introduced in the 1960s, further improved the manufacturers' ability to precisely control the relative longitudinal and torsional flex of skis.

But why did shorter skis with deep sidecuts not appear in a big way until the late 1990s? Did designers discover new materials? Were new manufacturing methods developed? Were special construction techniques invented? It seems the correct answer is none of the above. A few early attempts were made at producing shorter, more shapely skis, but they were victims of cultural inertia. Neither consumers nor the manufacturers' marketing departments liked them. And most designers seemed stuck in their thinking that a high-performance ski for an adult male had to be at least 200 centimeters long, which is too long for a shaped ski that will ski acceptably well.

Part of the impetus that finally got ski engineers moving in the right direction was the advent of deep sidecut snowboards capable of carving arcs that made expert skiers envious (figure 2.13). Another was the introduction of visionary skis like the Head Yahoo, Ivan Petkov's S Ski, the Kneissl Ergo and Elan's original SCX. They weren't commercial blockbusters, but did succeed in prying open the minds of skiers to the possibility that something better was possible, even if it looked goofy in the lift line. K2 was among the believers, and they produced the K2 Four, an advanced recreational ski. Bode Miller also believed, and he raced on a pair of K2 Fours to stunning results in the 1996 U.S. Junior Olympics and National Championships. Word of Bode's performance spread quickly among ski pros throughout the country, and within a few years we were all on the new shaped skis, skiing better and having more fun.

FIGURE 2.13 A good rider on a carving snowboard comes as close to making a perfectly carved turn as you can get. When skiers saw this in the mid 1990s, they said, "I want to be able to do that!" helping prompt the development of shaped skis. Rider: Lowell Hart.

Skidding, Oversteering, and Carving

Most skiers make most of their turns on a skidding ski: one that slips sideways as it moves forward. By making the tail slip faster than the tip, or *oversteering*, the skier makes the ski turn as it moves forward (figure 2.14). This is accomplished mainly through shifting pressure forward on a moderately edged ski or toward the tail on a relatively flat ski.

FIGURE 2.14   When a ski's tail slips sideways more than its tip as it moves forward, the ski is oversteering. All skiers rely on oversteering to shape many of their turns. When the skier puts pressure on the skis forebody, the lateral reaction force from the snow moves closer to the tip than the lateral force that the skier applies to the skis. This results in a torque that makes the skis turn. If the ski is flat enough, a similar effect can be produced by shifting pressure to the tail. Skier: Andy Gould.

Controlled oversteering is the essential mechanism for shaping turns in skiing. Skiers use oversteering from their first turns on skis until their last. As they become more adept, they learn to make turns with less oversteering and with smaller steering angles. This makes for smoother turns because a ski that's moving sideways doesn't absorb irregularities in the snow very well and is prone to catching outside edges. Oversteering also tends to feed on itself if it's not controlled well, resulting in a downhill stem at the end of the turn (figure 2.15).

Eventually, better skiers learn to carve their turns. Carving is a way of shaping turns smoothly and efficiently without oversteering, and with a minimal loss of speed because no skidding is involved. Skiers do most of their speed control through turning, either skidding or carving. The greater the steering angle of the ski under the foot—that is, the more skidding and oversteering—the more speed control comes from scraping and abrading the snow, which is inherently rough. The smaller the steering angle and the closer the skier gets to carving, the more speed control comes from the line the skier takes. By making turns that come completely around and across the fall line, the skier sheds speed like a cyclist coasting off a hill onto a flat road.

FIGURE 2.15   It's not hard for oversteering to get overdone in the last third of a turn, especially if the skier is too far forward. As the tail of this skier's downhill ski slides more, the ski slows down, and the skier's momentum puts him farther forward, making the tail slip even more. This is the cause of the chronic downhill stem that many skiers suffer. In most cases the solution is to bring the downhill foot forward a bit through the end of the turn to move pressure toward the middle of the ski. Skier: David N. Oliver.

When your ski is skidding through a turn, it has a constant sizeable steering angle directly under your feet. The resulting reaction force from the snow has a component pushing you toward the center of the turn, perpendicular to your direction of travel, which makes you turn. The force from the snow has another component that pushes straight back against your direction of travel, which slows you down.

What if you could eliminate that second component, leaving only the one that makes you turn? This is the conceptual basis for carving. The ski has an infinitesimal steering angle directly under your center of gravity when it's carving, but it comes from the ski's reverse camber, not from the ski being turned along its longitudinal axis. The ski continues to turn as it moves forward by banking against a curved groove in the snow that it carves for itself as it slides forward on that reverse camber. The groove is deep and substantial enough to prevent the ski from slipping sideways. The difference in the way a ski moves through oversteered and carved turns is shown in figure 2.16.

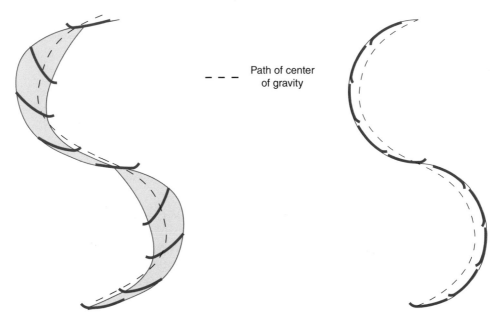

– – – Path of center
of gravity

FIGURE 2.16   The way a ski moves through an oversteered turn, such as the one on the left, is distinctly different from how it moves through a purely carved turn, such as the one on the right.

The groove and the way in which the ski and skier bank against it are conceptually similar to the way a bobsled banks against the wall of a turn in a bobsled track or a skateboarder turns against a curved wall in a skate park (figure 2.17). The physical mechanics of all three actions can be seen in the simple movement of a marble rolling in a circle around the inside of a large bowl (figure 2.18). The marble has momentum that would make it go in a straight line if not for the bowl, which exerts a force on the marble that pushes it toward the bowl's center (figure 2.19). That force arises because at every instant in time the marble is rolling into a surface that is at a minute angle to the direction it's going. In skiing terms, this angle is the bowl's steering angle in the sagittal plane at each instant, and is what makes the bowl push the ball out of its otherwise straight path.

FIGURE 2.17   A skateboarder in a skate park makes turns that closely resemble, at a physical level, carved turns made on skis.

FIGURE 2.18   A marble circling in a bowl provides a good model for a carved turn.

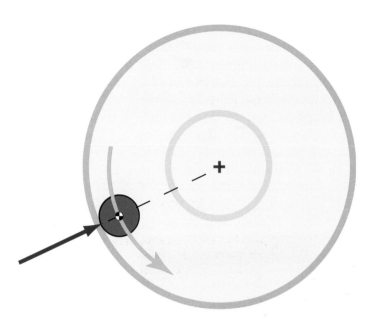

FIGURE 2.19 **The side of the bowl exerts a force on the marble directed at the bowl's center.**

FIGURE 2.20 **A ski that's carving cuts a groove in the snow. The resulting forces are much the same as those on the marble turning in the bowl and the skateboarder in the skate park.**

The marble corresponds to the ski and the skier in a carved turn, and the bowl corresponds to the curved groove carved in the snow by the ski. The forebody of the ski creates, in effect, the wall of the bowl (figure 2.20); as the part of the ski directly under the skier moves forward in the curved groove, it slides against a surface with a minute steering angle.

When a ski is carving perfectly, the entire reaction force from the snow is directed toward the center of the turn, perpendicular to the skier's direction of travel. There is no component that pushes opposite the skier's direction of travel (other than the small friction force between the snow and the ski's base). Consequently, the skier's momentum changes only in direction, not in magnitude.

Based on the radius of its sidecut and its longitudinal and torsional stiffness, any given ski is capable of carving arcs within a range of radii. What's the size of the smallest "bowl" that a modern ski carves in the snow? A good approximation for the carving radius of a torsionally stiff ski held at an edge angle of 45 degrees on hard snow is 70 percent of the ski's sidecut radius. At 60 degrees, the carving radius is 50 percent. More precisely, a ski with a sidecut radius R_{sc} held at an edge angle α and bent into reverse camber that brings the entire edge into contact with the snow will cut an arc with a radius $R = R_{sc} \cos \alpha$. This assumes the ski's sidecut is a section of a circle (which most are) and the ski doesn't flex dramatically in torsion. Some numbers for typical modern sidecuts and a typical slalom ski from the preshaped era are shown in table 2.1.

TABLE 2.1

Carving Radii for Typical Shaped and Traditional Non-Shaped Skis

Sidecut radius	Edge angle	Carved turn radius
17m (all-mountain ski)	45°	12 m (39 ft)
	60°	8.5 m (28 ft)
12m (high-performance carving ski)	45°	8.5 m (28 ft)
	60°	6 m (20 ft)
45m (traditional SL ski)	45°	31.5 m (103 ft)

These figures are approximate in part because they ignore torsional flexing.

An important chain of interrelated, circular dependencies is at work here, and is illustrated in figure 2.21:

- The carving radius is determined by the ski's reverse camber.
- The reverse camber is determined by the ski's sidecut and edge angle.
- The edge angle is determined primarily by the skier's inclination (the skier can also adjust the edge angle somewhat through angulation, described in chapter 8).
- The skier's inclination is determined entirely by his or her speed and the radius of the turn, as described in chapter 1.

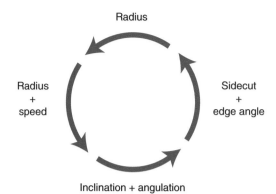

FIGURE 2.21 **A circular dependency exists between the radius of turn that a ski will carve, the sidecut of the ski, and the skier's speed.**

There's an interesting and important message here: At any given speed, a ski can carve turns perfectly within only a small range of radii, and the faster the speed, the shorter the radius of turn. This underscores the importance of matching the skis to the turns you want to make, if you want to carve your turns.

We can also now see that making a carved turn of a constant radius is nearly impossible, especially on a steep slope because the edge angle naturally increases as you come out of the fall line (because the slope falls away from you). It is, in fact, impossible to carve a straight traverse across a slope because of the ski's edge angle and sidecut.

Summary: Controlling the Ski's Self-Steering Effect

A good, versatile ski has many different turns built into it. If you only stand smack dab in the middle, though, you won't see too many of them. By judiciously adjusting the ski's platform angle, steering angle, edge angle, and the fore–aft distribution of pressure along its length, you can make the ski tighten or broaden its turn. You have these basic options for adjusting these components:

- If the ski is edged and engaged with the snow, increasing its edge angle by increasing inclination or angulation (described in chapter 8) can make the ski turn sharper because it allows the ski to bend into deeper reverse camber. Reducing inclination or angulation makes it turn less.
- Reducing the ski's platform and edge angles by increasing angulation makes it turn sharper, whereas reducing the angle increases the turn's radius. The biggest effects occur when the platform angle is in the neighborhood of 90 degrees.
- If the ski has a low edge angle or is in light contact with the snow, you can pivot it using techniques we'll look at in chapter 7.
- Moving pressure forward on a ski that is moderately edged but with a platform angle greater than 90 degrees will make it oversteer, increasing its overall steering angle and tightening the turn (up to the point that the steering angle is around 50 degrees). Moving back reduces oversteering.
- If the ski is only slightly edged, shifting pressure to the tail will also make it oversteer, increasing its overall steering angle. The ski will turn, but with problematic side effects. Although good skiers use this effect occasionally, many

average parallel skiers use it systematically to power their turns. This method is especially favored by skiers wishing to ski with their feet locked together.

- Moving pressure forward on an aggressively edged ski makes it turn more sharply. The shift makes the tip bend more, describing a tighter arc on the snow. Moving pressure forward also makes the tip bite more aggressively so that it dominates the ski's overall behavior. Note that the tail will not be carving the same arc as the forebody.

- If the ski is aggressively edged, shifting pressure toward the tail makes it go straighter. Moving pressure back takes both bend and bite out of the forebody, allowing the stiffer middle part of the ski to have a greater effect on the ski's track.

The ski's shape and flexural characteristics, managed through its three control angles and distribution of pressure fore and aft on the ski, give you the tools you need to shape turns and control speed. Modern shaped skis have not only made this easier but have given skiers the possibility of carving many of their turns—something few could do on earlier generations of equipment.

CHAPTER 3

Turn Anatomy 101

Al turns are not created equal. All share a common structure, but their components can look quite different from one to the next. In this chapter we examine the various species of turns and their similarities and differences, and introduce some terminology we will need later.

Phases of the Turn

Different things happen in different parts of every turn, and to give us a framework for their dissection, we need a clear vocabulary to refer to certain phases of the turn, namely *initiation*, *control*, *completion*, and *transition*. A single turn or a turn that begins from a traverse (however short) and ends with another has three phases: initiation, control, and completion. When turns are linked directly to one another, with no intervening traverse, the completion of the first flows seamlessly into the initiation of the next and together form a transition phase, as shown in figure 3.1.

Initiation

During the initiation you establish the initial steering angle needed to start the turn (discussed later in this chapter, p. 45). You do this so the snow, acting through

FIGURE 3.1 Turn phases. The transition encompasses the completion of one turn and the initiation of the next. Skier: Francois Bourque, Canada.

the ski, will make your path bend during the next phase of the turn, the control phase. In the initiation phase, you also align various body segments with each other and with your skis so that you can balance properly against the forces of the turn that will arise in the control phase. Your direction of travel doesn't change significantly in the initiation, which ends when the ski is solidly engaged with the snow.

The initiation phase is when you set the tone of the whole turn. You might float, dive, or ease into the initiation; you might hang back, hurry, or brace. The accuracy, dynamism, and commitment with which different skiers initiate their turns is a strong reflection of their ability levels.

Three things happen during the initiation:

1. Your balance axis inclines toward the inside of the new turn, relative to your outside ski, in anticipation of the centrifugal force you'll encounter in the upcoming control phase. In other words, your center of mass moves closer to the center of the new turn than your outside foot.

2. Your skis change edges. Strictly speaking, only one edge has to change. Whichever edge or edges were supporting the skier before the entry into the new turn, a different edge or edges will now do the work of making the turn happen.

3. At least one of your skis must establish a steering angle relative to your momentum. This could be as small as the angle provided by the ski's reverse camber when carving, as in figure 3.2, or a pivot of more than 40 degrees, as in figure 3.3.

FIGURE 3.2 When the size of the turn and the speed are right, the skier can initiate a turn just by rolling the ski on its edge and letting it carve. Skier: Aksel Lund Svindal, Norway.

FIGURE 3.3   To initiate a turn that's much sharper than the ski's carving radius, the skier may pivot her skis more than 40 degrees. Skier: Carol Levine.

Control

The control phase is where the snow makes you turn (figure 3.4). Significant lateral force between the ski and the snow makes your momentum's direction change, and the ski, because of its self-steering effect, turns itself as it moves forward. To take advantage of the ski's self-steering effect, you control the distribution of pressure fore and aft on the ski, as well as its platform angle and edge angle, to get the shape of turn you want. In short turns, especially on a steep slope, the control phase may be very short.

FIGURE 3.4   During the control phase the force from the snow changes the skier's direction of travel. The control phase of many modern slalom turns, like this one, is short and intense. Skier: Benjamin Raich, Austria.

Completion

During the completion phase you want to stop turning and either go into a traverse or start a turn in the other direction. To do this, you must eliminate the lateral force from the snow that was making you turn. You do this primarily by reducing your inclination into the turn and the ski's self-steering effect. These two actions occur together in a coordinated fashion. Reducing your inclination reduces the ski's edge angle, which reduces its self-steering effect. Reducing the self-steering effect reduces the ski's steering angle, which in turn reduces the lateral force from the snow, requiring less inclination to remain balanced.

In some turns, simply reducing the ski's edge angle will allow it to straighten out, putting the skier into a traverse. In many more dynamic turns, the skier may also encourage the ski to stop turning by shifting the distribution of pressure toward the tail, as shown in figure 3.5.

Another commonly used mechanism for completing the turn, especially when it will be linked closely with the next one, is to make the skis slow down or turn more tightly under the skier. Done properly, this has the effect of eliminating the skier's inclination, and hence ending the turn. Carried further, it can cause the skier to topple across the skis toward the inside of the next turn, beginning that turn's initiation phase.

FIGURE 3.5 Kathrin Zettel of Austria completes a slalom turn by moving the pressure on her outside ski from under the fall of her foot to the heel, while simultaneously reducing the ski's edge angle. This makes the ski run straight, releasing her from the turn.

Transition

Until they reach a certain level of skill, skiers execute turns that have distinct initiations and completions, separated by traverses. Advanced skiing starts when the traverse between a skier's parallel turns disappears and the completion of one turn and the initiation of the next merge into a seamless transition phase (figure 3.6). Now, instead of picturing a turn as going from traverse to traverse, it's often useful to view it as going from fall line to fall line, as many of the photomontages in this book are constructed. For an expert skier, the transition is a continuous succession of movements.

FIGURE 3.6   Aksel Lund Svindal of Norway melds the completion of one turn with the initiation of another in a fluid, seamless transition.

The transition begins when your body starts to be released from the lateral force of the turn and its momentum carries it in a straighter line than your feet are traveling. This is where the expert feels release and the illusion of acceleration. In the extreme, your skis pop from the snow, your feet fly to the outside of the new turn, and your body shoots down the hill in anticipation of the force that will develop when the skis engage the snow to make the next arc.

An important moment occurs during the transition when your center of gravity's path crosses that of your feet (figure 3.7). At this instant the skis are running straight and flat on the snow, making them easy to pivot. So the more accurately you can sense the crossover point, the more easily you can turn the skis without unweighting to disengage them from the snow. For the same reason, this is the moment when your pole plant can have the greatest turning effect (see Torque From the Pole Plant in chapter 7).

FIGURE 3.7   At the moment in the transition when the path of the center of gravity passes over that of the feet, the skis go flat. This is the moment to start steering them to their initial steering angle for the next turn. Skier: Laure Pequegnot, France.

The Virtual Bump

Because you make turns on a slope, the total force between you and the snow varies throughout every turn. Even on a perfectly smooth hill, the effect of making turns is just like skiing through bumps. The better the skis hold and the tighter the turn, the greater the effect. In a sharply carved turn made on a smooth slope, for instance, you will feel light at the top of the turn and heavy at the bottom. This is because the gradient the skis are on changes through the course of the turn in the same way it does when you ski over one bump and into another.

On the left of figure 3.8, you can see the track of two idealized turns. The right of that figure shows the gradient on which the skis are running at each instant in those turns. At the beginning, the skis are across the fall line, on a relatively flat grade. As the skier approaches the fall line, the grade becomes steeper and steeper, and as the skier turns out of the fall line, the skis come onto a flatter and flatter grade. The gradient traced by the skis, as shown on the right of figure 3.8, looks just like the profile traced by a skier running through bumps.

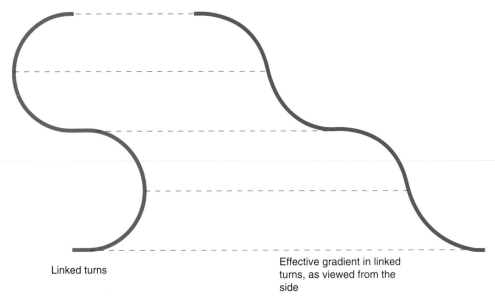

Linked turns

Effective gradient in linked turns, as viewed from the side

FIGURE 3.8   As a skier moves through turns on a smooth slope, the effective gradient changes as if the skier were skiing through bumps.

Another way to look at the same phenomenon is shown in figure 3.9. Gravity always points in the same direction. At the start of the turn, what little centrifugal force there is points the other way, making you feel light. At the end of the turn, the two forces are pointing in nearly the same direction, making you feel heavy. In between, the total force you feel builds continuously. Again, this is just like skiing first into the trough between two bumps, and into another bump at the end of the turn.

Adding to the effect is the fact that when going from one turn to another, you go from being inclined to one side of your feet to being inclined the other way. This action, shown in figure 3.10 on page 42, tosses you upward just as a bump would. The total effect, which I call the *virtual bump*, plays a fundamental role in all of advanced skiing. Figure 3.11, also on page 42, shows a World Cup slalom skier flexing to absorb the virtual bump between two tightly carved turns on a smooth slope.

FIGURE 3.9 Gravity and centrifugal force interact through the course of the turn to make the skier feel lighter at the start and heavier at the end, just as if he or she were skiing in bumps. Skier: Benjamin Raich, Austria.

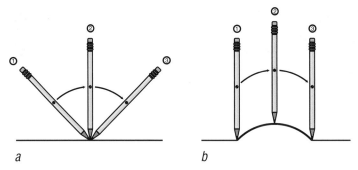

FIGURE 3.10   The change of inclination a skier undergoes when moving from one turn to another is something like what happens to this pencil—its center of gravity gets projected upward along the way, as if passing over a bump. Figures 3.11 and 6.20 on page 104 are good examples of this in skiing.

FIGURE 3.11   Janica Kostelic of Croatia flexes at the knees and waist in the transition between these turns, yet her body is lifted because she's skiing over a virtual bump. Although the hill is smooth, the dynamics of the turn have the same effect on the skier as a mogul. For more on Janica Kostelic, see page 44.

Just as if she were skiing in moguls, she is most fully extended in the middle of the turn and most flexed in the transition. The effect of the virtual bump makes it easier to start a turn from the end of the previous turn, rather than from a traverse, and it's one of the tools experienced skiers use to make skiing less work when they are tired or just want to relax and cruise. For the world-class racer, the effect reaches magnitudes that make it formidable and potentially disastrous. How to exploit and control the virtual bump is addressed in chapters 6 and 9.

Types of Turns

I'm going to start with an intentional oversimplification and say that there are three types of turns: skidded turns, checked turns, and carved turns. In truth, these are idealizations that seldom, if ever, occur in their pure forms. Still, most turns are dominated by the characteristics of one or another of these three basic types. In practice, very few turns are perfectly carved, and most turns that end with a check have a control phase that involves some skidding and possibly carving. So as we consider carved, skidded, and checked turns, keep in mind that there's some overlap in nearly every turn we make.

Skidded Turns

A ski making a skidded turn moves sideways as it moves forward—the kind of turn a car racing on a dirt track makes. The skid makes use of the oversteering characteristics of skis, discussed in chapter 2, to make the skis turn themselves as they move forward. The middle of the ski engages the snow at a steering angle to the skier's momentum in the transverse plane, and the snow pushes back to turn or slow the skier down (figure 3.12). The component that acts perpendicular to the skier's momentum is that portion of the snow's force that makes the skier turn.

The more a turn is skidded, the less efficient it is and the more the skier's speed and momentum is scrubbed away. The less smooth the turn is, too, because the ski doesn't absorb irregularities and shocks nearly as well when it hits them sideways as when it encounters them with its tip.

Along with being easy to execute, skidded turns are an obvious way to control speed, and that's why most skiers rely on these turns, even on modern equipment that's designed to carve. This is not to say that skidding is categorically bad. All skiers, including the best in the world, do it frequently. Skidding with purpose and finesse is every bit as important a skill as carving, and has gotten something of a bad rap since shaped skis have become popular.

Carved Turns

In an ideal carved turn, the ski never moves sideways while it's engaged with the snow (figure 3.13). This is the sort of turn you make on a bicycle, a skateboard, or skates. When a ski is carving perfectly, employing the mechanics described in chapter 2, it has a very small steering angle in the sagittal plane only, and the snow's force on the skier has no slowing component: The entire force is perpendicular to the skier's direction of travel at every point in the turn. Carved turns are efficient and stable, two qualities that give them a distinctly seductive feel. Once you discover them, it's easy to become addicted. But in the real world, virtually all the turns we make have some slowing component, and the distinction between what we call carved and skidded turns is not absolute.

Before the widespread appearance of shaped skis in the late 1990s, true carving was an ideal not often realized. The dramatic improvements in skis during the intervening years have put carved turns within the reach of more and more skiers and added remarkable vitality to the sport. However, most turns made by most skiers still involve a fair amount of skidding.

FIGURE 3.12 Skidded turns. The skis are at a large steering angle throughout the entire control phase. Compare these steering angles with those in figure 3.13.

FIGURE 3.13 The best racers distinguish themselves by their ability to carve, making many of their turns with virtually no skidding. Skier: Kathrin Zettel, Austria.

Janica Kostelic

Janica Kostelic, now retired, is unquestionably one of the greatest skiers, male or female, of all time. Her record includes three overall World Cup titles; three slalom titles; six Olympic medals, four of them gold (the most ever by a woman); and five World Championship gold medals. Kostelic is one of only three women to win World Cup races in all five disciplines, and she holds the record for the highest number of World Cup points scored in a single season. She did all this despite being sidelined several times by injuries. During her career, her only consistently serious competition for the overall title was Anja Paerson, the great Swedish skier.

Kostelic's fundamental technique was so sound that she could win runs without taking every possible risk. That technique has made her a model not only for aspiring competitors, but for all skiers. It was perfectly adapted to the new world of shaped skis, possibly because she did not develop through a strong national association's program with an entrenched approach to skiing. Instead, she and her brother Ivica, himself a preeminent World Cup racer, developed under the tutelage of their father in Croatia. A family of modest means, the Kostelics forged their own way to the World Cup.

Among Janica's strongest technical strengths was her ability to maintain contact with the snow through the transition with perfect flexion moves so that she could get pressure on the edge early in the turn. She also understood when and how to use her inside ski to the best advantage. Her technique, coupled with the precision of her line judgment, enabled her to ski consistently clean runs without needing to make recoveries or line corrections, as evidenced by the seven consecutive World Cup slaloms she won in the 2000-01 season.

Until late in her career, when she skied with chronic back pain but still won races, Janica Kostelic's consummate technique was punctuated with an element that I've always appreciated: She smiled when she raced.

Checked Turns

In a checked turn, the skier sets the edges sharply at a large steering angle at the turn's completion. The skis slow dramatically, but the momentum of the skier's body carries it across the feet into the next turn, pulling the skis along with it (figure 3.14). If you visualize how a Slinky toy marches down a flight of stairs, you can grasp how checked turns work.

FIGURE 3.14   Checked turns are essentially a series of linked edgesets. There may be a bit of carving leading up to an edgeset, but it will be brief. Skier: Ron LeMaster.

Photo courtesy of Bob Barnes

This is the sort of short radius turn an expert makes on a steep hill when speed control is critical. In the extreme, this style of turning feels like hopping down a flight of stairs, something like that Slinky toy.

With the edgeset, the skis almost stop. Then, to the extent that the hip and knee extensors—mostly the thigh and buttock muscles—contract, the motion of the skier's center of gravity will slow, too. The force from the snow produced by the edgeset has a large slowing component, although the skis might skid very little. The momentum lost by the skier is transferred to the earth itself.

The Initial Steering Angle

In chapter 2, table 2.1 illustrated the size of turns that can be carved with typical modern skis at different edge angles. An edge angle of 45 degrees is achievable by a very good, technically proficient skier. Experts who really know their stuff are capable in certain circumstances of holding edge angles of 60 degrees or so. Higher angles are, at this time, the domain of high-level competitive skiers. A technically strong skier on an all-mountain ski can probably carve a turn with a radius of about 12 meters, or a bit less than 40 feet. On a full-on carving ski, the radius tightens to about 8.5 meters, or 28 feet.

These are big turns—bigger than many of the turns a skier makes in a day of skiing. They are the sorts of turn depicted in figure 3.15*a*, using our model of a marble rolling around in a bowl. In this case, we have two bowls of a radius that correspond to the ski's carving radius. The bowls are aligned so they match up perfectly, and the marble never encounters a steering angle larger than the infinitesimally small angle presented by the bowl's curve. This provides a model for two turns that correspond perfectly with the carving radius of a ski.

Partially Carved Turns

As I've said, many turns a skier wants to make are quite a bit smaller than the carving radius achievable even with deep-cut carving skis. We can make these turns with little or no skidding through what could be called *partial carving*.

Figure 3.15*b* illustrates turns in which the marble must change direction more quickly than the curve the bowls alone will produce. Each time the marble leaves one bowl, it hits the side of the next at an angle, and there's a component of the reaction force from the bowl that reduces the marble's momentum. But as soon as the marble is rolling along the wall of the next bowl, it's immediately carving again, and no more momentum is lost through the rest of the turn.

This second scenario provides an idealized description of how you can make a partially carved turn that's smaller than the natural turning radius of the ski. You start by pivoting the ski to an initial steering angle in the transverse plane from which the ski is made to carve an arc of a radius that's within its range. This is, in fact, how many carved turns are made, both by recreational skiers and World Cup racers.

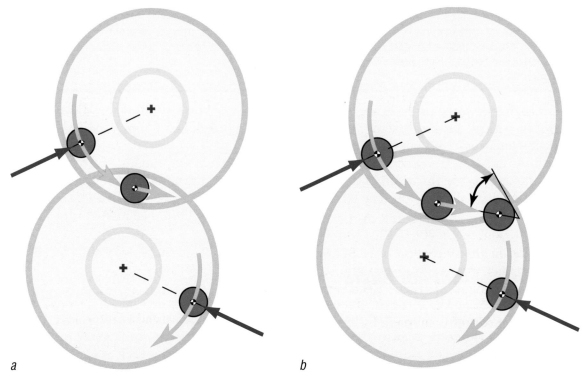

a *b*

FIGURE 3.15   *(a)* When the bowls line up just right, the marble can make perfectly linked arcs by going from bowl to bowl. For a ski to make perfectly carved linked turns, the turns must match in the same way the carving radius of the ski at the speed the skier is going. *(b)* When the bowls are closer together than in figure 3.15*a*, the marble hits the wall of the second bowl at an angle, then rolls along an arc from that point. A ski can make partially carved turns smaller than its carving radius by being pivoted to an initial steering angle corresponding to the angle at which the marble hits the wall of the second bowl.

Note that the angle between the ski and the fall line is not the issue here. Rather, it's the angle between the ski and your direction of travel (that is, your momentum) that counts. If you're traveling in a shallow traverse, the ski can have a significant steering angle well before it reaches the fall line, and so can generate a useful turning force. If, on the other hand, you're making short turns that don't stray far from the fall line, not much will happen until the ski is in the fall line or perhaps past it.

How you go about establishing that initial steering angle is a key element of every system of ski instruction. When you ski in a wedge, each ski always has a steering angle (figure 3.16). All you need to do to initiate a turn is to make one ski dominant, either by putting a majority of your weight on it, or by twisting it to a larger steering angle than the other ski.

FIGURE 3.16   In a wedge, the skis are always at a steering angle, one in either direction.

As skiers get better, they learn ways, some of them subtle, to guide both skis in parallel to an initial steering angle. Their purpose is always the same: to get the midbody of the ski to a steering angle that extracts the lateral force from the snow that turns them in the direction they want to go.

The Size of the Initial Steering Angle

How big an initial steering angle do you need for a particular turn? That depends on the turn and whether you want to carve as much of it as you can. The sharper the turn, the greater the initial steering angle. Small initial steering angles provide a progressive buildup of force from the snow and a smooth entry into the turn but are inappropriate for short turns, especially on steep terrain. A large initial steering angle makes for a dramatic buildup of reaction force. Recall, too, that when the size of the steering angle gets beyond a certain point, you get more speed control and less direction change.

Turns in which the ski follows its edge from start to finish—that is, turns with little or no initial steering angle—are fine on broad, groomed runs that don't require you to turn in any particular place. More and more of our skiing terrain seems to be going in that direction, too. But when you seek more challenging terrain, you'll need greater initial steering angles. Large initial steering angles are necessary, for instance, for short turns on steep slopes. In the sort of turn made by extreme skiers in very steep couloirs, the skis are pivoted nearly 180 degrees before they engage the snow.

Partially carved turns are the bread and butter of high-performance skiing on hard snow. Current practice among World Cup slalom and giant slalom skiers is to start carving as early as possible in the turn, which in slalom and giant slalom is usually somewhere around the fall line (figures 3.17 and 3.18).

FIGURE 3.17   In this turn, Mario Matt starts carving slightly before the fall line after establishing an initial steering angle of about 40 degrees. For more on Matt, see page 154.

So, how do you know what the initial steering angle should be for any given turn? The way an expert at carving judges the initial steering angle is similar to the way an archer aims an arrow. When aiming at a target, an archer doesn't point the arrow directly at the bull's-eye. Knowing that the arrow will follow a curved path from the bow to the target, the archer aligns the arrow with that curve at the point where it meets the bow (figure 3.19).

FIGURE 3.18   Ted Ligety of the United States starts a giant slalom turn on a steep pitch with a large initial steering angle. The skis don't engage the snow until they're almost in the fall line, having been redirected over 50 degrees. For more on Ligety, see page 134.

FIGURE 3.19   The dotted line is the ballistic curve the arrow must follow if it is to hit the bull's-eye. To aim accurately, the archer lines the arrow up with that curve.

The skier's problem is similar to the archer's, and world-class racers have developed their own version of the archer's solution. Before starting a turn, racers know where they want the turn to end and in what direction they want to be going at that point (figure 3.20*a*). Knowing from experience how sharp an arc they can carve, they in effect see that arc on the snow, beginning at the turn's intended exit point and progressing back up the hill (figure 3.20*b*). They then initiate the turn by pivoting the ski until it is aligned with that arc at the point it intersects their current path, and establishing the initial steering angle. When the ski lines up with the arc, the racer engages it with the snow and carves to the turn's completion (figure 3.20*c*).

Line selection is complicated by the pitch of the hill. Because of the pitch, the ski's edge angle will always be smallest early in the turn and get progressively greater until the turn's completion (figure 3.21). Because the ski's edge angle determines its carving radius, the turn's radius will naturally get tighter as the turn proceeds. The steeper the hill, the greater the effect. It can be mitigated somewhat by carving with the forebody early in the turn and moving back on the ski coming through the bottom, but the fact remains that nice, circular arcs just aren't possible on slopes with much pitch.

Becoming deft with skis or arrows requires learning the shapes of the curves they make. In archery, the curves vary with the pull of the bow, the distance to the target, the wind, and so on. In skiing, too, many factors contribute, including the shape, stiffness, and condition of the skis; the size of the turn; the skier's speed; the slope of the hill; the character of the snow; and others.

Many skiers start their turns with excessive steering angles. They fling their skis sideways into the turn, resulting in a barely controlled power slide. By oversteering the ski from the start, they never give it a chance to slice, but instead make it scrape. Unfortunately, most of these skiers never develop an appreciation for fitting their skis to a round, smooth arc. Skiers who insist on skiing on only steeps and moguls are especially prone to learning only to pivot and skid. They need to understand that making many turns of all sizes at all speeds on smooth, moderate terrain is essential to the development of well-rounded ski technique. I often seek out smooth, gentle runs and practice making slow, clean, carved turns. This is a great exercise to work on balance, control, and snow sensitivity.

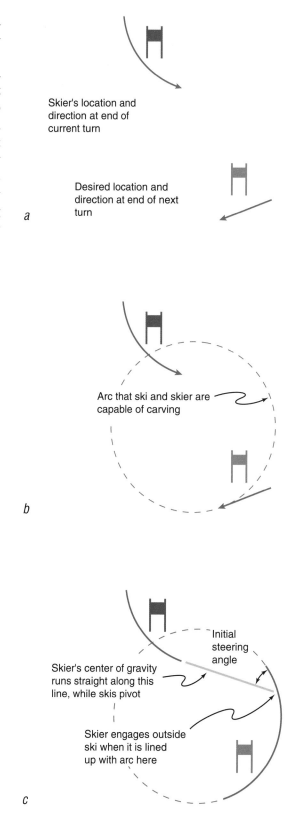

FIGURE 3.20 *(a)* A carved turn starts with identifying the intended exit point and the desired direction of travel when the skier gets there. *(b)* The skier visualizes the curve that the skis can carve to the turn's exit point. *(c)* The skier pivots the outside ski to align it with the arc it can carve, then carves to the turn's exit point.

FIGURE 3.21   Massimiliano Blardone and Benjamin Raich, who finished first and second in this run, less than seven hundredths of a second apart, select slightly different lines for this turn but with the same initial steering angle. Notice that because the radius and speed of their turns are virtually identical, so is their angle of inclination into the turn.

Controlled skidding and slipping are required in many turns to achieve a desired line and speed. Still, the extent to which the skidding can be reduced generally makes the turn smoother, more controlled, and more enjoyable. And because it's fair to say that skidding comes far more naturally to skiers, carving skills are the ones requiring deliberate study and practice.

PART II

Techniques:
Controlling Your Interaction With the Snow

Too many skiers have the notion that there's some approved menu of correct turns that are to be executed using a narrowly choreographed sequence of movements. They are otherwise good skiers who know how to perform a variety of fundamental movements, but they combine them in rote patterns that impose the skiers' technique on the hill. They know the foxtrot, so that's the dance they do.

Really good skiers mix, match, and vary their movements on the fly in response to the shape and texture of the snow, the pitch of the hill, the turns they want to make, and the effects they want to feel. We use words like *touch* and *feel* to describe the way these skiers come down the hill, and when we see them ski by, they communicate a pleasure that we want to feel ourselves.

A good way to become a really good skier is to learn to make those fundamental movements in isolation. Once you can make them cleanly and independently of the other movements, you're prepared to produce the turn of the moment, rather than the turn of the textbook.

What makes these movements fundamental is that they control some basic interaction between the skis, the snow, and ourselves. We move forward and backward over the skis, for example, to maintain stability fore and aft and to control the distribution of force and pressure along the length of each ski. We edge or flatten the ski to control its grip on the snow. In technical terms, the fundamental movements of skiing are about controlling the magnitude of the force the snow exerts on us, the direction it pushes us, and how we arrange our bodies to balance against it.

The chapters in this part of the book are about those fundamental movements. I divide them into five categories:

■ Fore and aft movements. These are movements that control the position of the skier's balance axis along the length of the skis, affecting the distribution of force forward and backward along them and hence the skis' turning behavior and the skier's stability.

■ Up and down movements. These are movements that control the distance between the skier's center of gravity and the skis along the skier's balance axis, affecting the total amount of force the snow exerts on the skier.

■ Movements that turn the skis. These are movements that control the direction the skis are pointed relative to the direction the skier is going—the skis' overall steering angle in the transverse plane.

■ Edging movements. These are movements that control the angle of the ski's edge relative to the force on it from the snow—the ski's platform angle, which determines how well the ski holds—and the alignment of the hips, knees, and ankles in relation to that force. These movements also fine-tune the ski's edge angle and thereby its carving radius.

■ Lateral balancing movements. These are movements that control the skier's inclination into the turn, affecting balance against turning and slowing forces from the snow, and the ski's edge angle. These movements are also a critical ingredient in linking turns.

The posture of your body when you're skiing—the relative arrangement of your limbs and joints and the muscles that drive them—determines the degree of ease or difficulty with which you can make these fundamental movements while balancing against the forces of skiing. This important topic is covered in chapter 4.

Because so much of ski technique is about manipulating and balancing against the skis, your skiing can be no better than the equipment that connects you with them: your boots. That connection is so important that we devote a chapter to the subtleties of boot fit and alignment.

There's a difference between *what* good coaches and instructors teach, and *how* they teach it. The first is technique; the second is teaching methodology. Suppose you want a skier to edge the skis early in the turn by rotating the outside knee inward, and at the same time put pressure on the outside ski's forebody by bending the outside ankle. These are techniques. You can simply say, "Drive your knee into the turn." This is a teaching method, which most skiers learn better from than an on-hill recitation of the technical details.

Good teaching and coaching depend on good methods of that kind. Understanding why and how the methods work depends on understanding technique. Understanding technique will help you apply the teaching methods you pick up from others, including the ones in this book, and help you develop your own. So that you know whether I'm presenting technique or methodology in the chapters that follow, look for these clues: When I talk about doing an exercise or what you might feel when you make a particular movement, you should generally take that as methodology. The detailed descriptions of movements are generally descriptions of technique.

When you take the information and images from this part of the book out to the slopes and experiment with your technique, keep the following tips in mind:

- Be willing to ski less than your best. You seldom do new things as well as the ones you've already got grooved, even if what you've got grooved aren't the best things you could be doing. Try new things, work at the things you don't do well, and accept that you'll feel uncoordinated and uncomfortable for a while.

- Exaggerate. A new movement or change in stance will feel bigger than it is. And if there's something you haven't been doing enough of, you have to know what it feels like to do too much before you can know what's right.

- Simplify the training environment. Work on skills in terrain and snow that are relatively easy so you can focus on the tasks at hand.

4 CHAPTER

Alignment and Stance

FIGURE 4.1   Each skier has a gestalt that an experienced instructor or coach will quickly pick up. This personal signature expresses how comfortable the skier is, how in tune with the snow and terrain, and how able to act at will or react to the unexpected. We rely on a single word to describe this collection of individual technical details and how they fit together: *stance*. What we look for when we assess a skier's stance is the alignment of the key parts of the skier's body, both with the forces of skiing and with each other. Skier: David N. Oliver.

As skis have become more sophisticated, the forces skiers develop in turns have increased, which means proper alignment and stance are now more important than ever. Just as there are safe and unsafe ways to align your body when lifting heavy objects, there are safe and unsafe ways to align it when skiing. Whenever you're in a flexed, athletic stance, you're depending on certain muscles to prevent your body from collapsing. When bending to lift a heavy box, you bend at the knees rather than at the waist. That's because bending at the knees supports the load with your thigh and buttock muscles, whereas bending at the waist puts unsafe demands on the muscles of your lower back. In skiing, too, an effective stance is based on the best alignment of muscles and bones to balance the forces of skiing so that you can remain strong, supple, and efficient as you move through turns and variations in terrain and snow (figure 4.1).

The alignment of your body segments strongly influences your range of motion, too, and your ability to accurately balance and control the edges of your skis as you make all the movements described in the subsequent chapters of the book.

General Alignment and Stance Principles

A few biomechanical principles will help us understand what makes for good alignment and stance. One or more of them underpin every topic in this chapter and every facet of technique in this book. Taken on their own, they are basic principles of good skiing.

The Balance Axis is the Reference for Alignment. Balancing against the forces of skiing means balancing along the balance axis, defined in chapter 1. While gravity plays a part in where the balance axis is, it's only one of several factors, so a true vertical line is not of much use for us here.

Each Segment of the Body Balances on the One Below It. Your torso balances on the heads of your femurs. Your torso, hips, and upper legs balance on top of your knees. Your torso, hips, and legs balance on your ankles and feet. When you're in a turn on firm snow, most of your body's mass is balanced on one leg, knee, and ankle. Depending on your alignment, different muscles are called on at each of the major joints to do the work of supporting and balancing the body segments above it. Good alignment enlists the strongest and best muscles.

The Upper and Lower Body Must Work Independently. The lower body—the legs and feet—plays a distinctly different role from the upper body (that portion from the hips up). You ski with your legs. You balance with your upper body. On average, about 65 percent of a person's mass is contained in the upper body and about 35 percent in the legs and feet. Looking at a skier from the front, the center of gravity is located somewhere just above the hips. As a result, small movements of the upper body have a disproportionately large effect on a skier's balance and the distribution of force and pressure on the skis. That's why the best skiers keep their upper bodies quiet. They put their torso over the part of the ski they want to apply force to, and they don't move it much. If they want more force on the outside ski, the upper body goes over that ski. If they want even pressure between their skis, the upper body is in the middle.

The best skiers use their legs, whose joints have many degrees of freedom, to manipulate the skis underneath the massive, quiet upper body. The legs turn the skis, control their edges, and adjust their fore–aft position relative to the skier's center of gravity.

The Legs Must Work Independently. Racers have always known that the functionally best technique in skiing is based on using their legs independently. Like the independent suspension on each of the wheels of a high-performance sports car, each leg must respond in its own way to variations in the shape of the snow surface. When you're in a turn, you apply force to the inside edge of one foot and the outside edge of the other, and your inclination requires your inside leg to be bent more than your outside leg. Any element of stance that prevents them from being able to do their own thing hinders you.

The Hips Must Be Stable and Well Controlled. Some of the best coaching methods focus on the hips: "Move your hips forward into the turn." "Stabilize your hips." "Keep your hips over your feet." The hips play a central role in skiing because they are, literally, central to your body. The hips are where the upper and lower body meet, and if the upper and lower body are to work independently, the muscles around the hips must constantly contract and relax in a coordinated fashion to adjust your balance and manipulate your skis while adapting to changes in external forces. These muscles support and balance the mass of the upper body over the heads of the femurs, and good alignment in the midbody is largely a matter of arranging the hips in the sagittal, frontal, and transverse planes so that the strongest, most effective muscles are used.

The hips are also near your center of gravity. So it's more than poetic license to say that your body revolves around them. If they move erratically, your entire body moves that way, and your center of gravity with it. Be careful, though, not to confuse your hips with your center of gravity, because it's the latter that determines your state of balance, not the former.

A lot of skiing happens in the ball-and-socket joints where the femurs meet the pelvis. Some of their movements are controlled by the biggest muscles in the body, and their three degrees of freedom and range of articulation give them great versatility. Having so many options for movement provides you with many ways to accomplish any particular task, but only a few of them are optimal. Consequently, the alignment of the hips in relation to the legs and upper body, which is one of the main subjects in this chapter, plays a central role in ski technique.

You Must Be Able to Act and React From a Neutral Stance. Skiers can learn a lot about stance by watching athletes in other sports. A football linebacker defending against an oncoming opponent provides a good model for a skier's neutral, home-base stance. The linebacker needs to be in a posture from which he can move in any direction as quickly and powerfully as possible, and take a hit without getting knocked out of balance. This stance is flexed at all the major joints. The hands are at the same height, about halfway between the hips and shoulder. The athlete's balance is on the balls of his feet. With a couple of tweaks—the stance is generally narrower and the balance maybe a hair farther back—this is the basic neutral stance of an athletic skier.

Each of the movements of skiing has its own range. A skier's vertical movement, for example, can range from standing almost bolt upright to a low tuck or lower. There's a point within each of these ranges that we can think of as its neutral point: a place the skier will go to to be ready to move in one direction or another within that range. The collection of all those neutral points defines a skier's overall neutral stance or home base.

Good skiers continually pass through the neutral points of various movements when they're skiing, but they don't linger there, and there are few moments in dynamic skiing when all movement patterns are in their various neutral points at the same time.

Alignment in the Sagittal Plane

When you move fore and aft or up and down, you flex and extend joints in the sagittal plane (figure 4.2). So the elements of alignment we'll discuss here are concerned mostly with your ability to move and balance in those directions accurately and through an ample range.

FIGURE 4.2 The skier viewed in the sagittal plane. Skier: Jerry Berg.

Center of Gravity

We often talk about having your balance, or your center of gravity, "over your feet." Sounds simple enough, doesn't it? But it's not. At the heart of the issue is what "over" means. It doesn't mean that your center of gravity and feet must be aligned with respect to gravity. It means they must be aligned with respect to the balance axis, as defined in chapter 1 (figures 1.17 and 1.18 on p. 17). Recall that the balance axis goes through your center of gravity and is perpendicular to the bottom of your skis, and is seldom aligned with gravity (figure 1.8 on p. 9). So when a coach says your balance is over your feet, that means the balance axis falls somewhere between the balls of your feet and the back of your arch when viewed in the sagittal plane.

That's the essential rule of fore–aft balance, and it implies some interesting things about your hips and shoulders. To be in a flexed, athletic stance, your shoulders must be ahead of your hips. Furthermore, your shoulders will be ahead of your center of gravity and your hips behind it. And unless you're standing pretty tall, your shoulders will be ahead of your feet and your hips will be behind them, with respect to the balance axis, which is the reference of alignment that really matters. There's a tried and true coaching method that says, "Keep your hips over your feet." It's an effective method, but it's technically inaccurate, as Lindsey Vonn shows in figure 4.3 and Aksel Lund Svindal shows in figure 4.4.

FIGURE 4.3 Lindsey Vonn of the United States, currently the best female skier in the world, is in perfect balance at 70+ mph (113+ km/h) because her center of gravity is over her feet, as defined by the balance axis. Note that her hips are behind her feet and her shoulders are ahead of them. For more on Vonn, see page 103.

FIGURE 4.4 Aksel Lund Svindal's balance is rock solid through these well-carved turns. When he flexes, his hips move back, but his shoulders come forward, keeping his center of gravity in the right place: over his feet.

Lower-Leg Angle

The angle of the skier's lower leg in the sagittal plane controls fore–aft balance more than that of any other part of the body, and the forward angle of the boot's cuff determines the lower-leg angle's neutral point. Every degree of change in the angle of the lower leg moves your center of gravity forward or backward about 10 times as much as a similar change in the angle at which you bend forward at the waist. Changing the leg's angle by just 5 degrees moves your center of gravity about 3 inches (7.6 cm)—about the distance from the middle of your arch to the ball of your foot.

Because ski boots don't allow the ankles much range of motion in the sagittal plane, the skier can't adjust that angle much while skiing. So finding a boot with the right neutral point, the right range, and the right stiffness of forward flex is fundamental to good balance fore and aft.

The cuffs of ski boots are pitched forward at an angle, called *forward lean,* so that the skier's center of gravity can stay over the feet while flexing into a low stance (figure 4.5). Too little forward lean causes the skier to lose balance to the rear when flexing deeply (figure 4.6), which is a far more common problem than too much forward lean. Too much forward lean might require the skier to adopt a vertical neutral point that's too low for comfort, too upright at the waist for smooth, vertical motion, or too far forward on the skis. World-class racers and mogul skiers (conditioned skiers for whom the ability to ski effectively in a low stance is important) typically ski in boots with enough forward lean to allow them to flex very deeply. The subject of forward lean, including how to measure how much you need and how to adjust your boots to get it, is covered in depth in chapter 10.

FIGURE 4.5   When the skier's lower legs are pitched forward sufficiently by the boots, the skier can flex deeply and still remain in balance fore and aft. Skier: Jerry Berg.

FIGURE 4.6   This skier can't keep her center of gravity over her feet as she absorbs this bump because her lower legs are not tilted forward enough by her boots. Compare the relative lengths of her femurs and torso to those of the skier in figure 4.5. That, along with the shape of her calf muscles and relative distribution of mass in her body, means that her boots need more forward lean. Skier: Annie Black.

Aksel Lund Svindal

Aksel Lund Svindal has continued a trend in World Cup athletes since the tour's inception in the late 1960s: The best overall skiers have gotten bigger. Both Svindal and Bode Miller, the last two skiers to have won the overall World Cup more than once, are almost 10 percent taller and fully a third heavier than Killy, Schranz, and Thoeni, the first three champions.

Another more recent trend is that in the last decade, the overall title on the men's side has generally gone to competitors who have excelled in speed events, which favor bigger athletes. The World Cup has more downhill and super G events, and fewer slaloms and giant slaloms. Compounding this effect is the fact that slalom and giant slalom have, by their nature, more uncertainty and variability in their results. The best skiers in the technical events seldom get on the podium with the consistency of those in the speed disciplines.

In these respects, Svindal has a lot going for him. He's big, and he's very good at the speed events, as well as giant slalom. He is very controlled in the movements he makes to stay in contact with the snow through the transition, so that, in turns where others get jacked from the snow, Svindal's skis stay close to the ground, ready to engage the next turn and work its arc. His shoulders are always ahead of his hips, even when he moves pressure back to the heel of his foot, and he rarely gets stretched out with his feet ahead of him going into the turn.

Svindal's personality is one of his biggest competitive assets. He just doesn't seem to get rattled. He steps up in big events, competes well in tough conditions, and can return from setbacks as well as anyone, if not better. In December 2006, in a training run for the Birds of Prey downhill at Beaver Creek, one of the most difficult courses in the world, Svindal uncharacteristically made a terrible error at the takeoff of the Golden Eagle jump, the biggest on the course. Flying through the air at around 70 mph, Svindal flipped over backward, landing 200 feet (60 m) down the hill on his shoulders and neck. He suffered broken bones in his face and a large gash in his groin, probably from his ski. After missing the entire remainder of the season, Aksel returned to Beaver Creek the next December for the first downhill of the year and won. He also won the super G contested the next day on the same hill, and placed third in the third race of the weekend, a giant slalom.

That year Svindal went on to win the overall World Cup title, as he had the year before his injury, edging out Benjamin Raich of Austria with 1,009 points to Raich's 1,007, the smallest margin in World Cup history.

Continuing a long tradition of exceptional Norwegian skiers, Aksel Lund Svindal is a model of technique as well as competitive spirit, and we can expect to see him on the top step of many podiums in the future.

Lead

In a parallel turn, lead is the distance the inside ski is ahead of the outside when viewed in the sagittal plane. Back in the 1950s and 1960s, skiers were often taught to deliberately shove the inside ski ahead of the other one when starting a turn, and many thought that the lead change a good skier made going from one turn to the next was a fundamental movement of good turns. This is no longer widely thought. The inside ski does lead the outside ski in virtually all good turns made on alpine ski equipment, but it's the result of other movements rather than a deliberate act of advancing the inside ski for its own sake.

When you're inclined into a turn, your inside leg must be bent more than your outside leg, as if you were standing in a traverse (figure 4.7). In particular, the inside femur is articulated more in the hip than the outside femur, which brings your inside knee forward of the outside knee in the sagittal plane. Because the ski boot allows little flex of the inside ankle, your inside foot must come forward with the knee, establishing the inside ski's lead (figures 4.8 and 4.9).

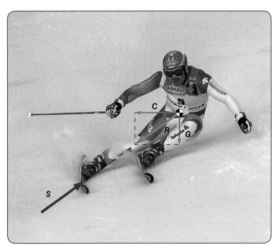

a   *b*

FIGURE 4.7   The skier's inclination into the turn has a similar effect on his stance to that of standing on a slope: The inside leg is flexed in the hip more than the outside leg. Skier: Didier Cuche, Switzerland.

a   *b*

FIGURE 4.8   *(a)* A person wearing shoes can flex the femur in the pelvis without the foot coming forward because the ankle can flex freely. *(b)* A person wearing ski boots can't, however, and the foot must come forward.

FIGURE 4.9 As Marlies Schild of Austria inclines steeply into the turn and her inside leg flexes at the hip, her inside ski moves ahead of her outside ski.

The more inclination you have, the greater the difference in flex between your inside and outside femurs, and the more lead your inside ski will have. The lead is also increased by the degree to which your hips are rotated in the transverse plane (about the balance axis) toward the outside of the turn, a subject we'll address in our discussion of counter (see p. 73).

For decades, instructors said that a line drawn between the tips of the skis should be parallel to a line drawn between the hip joints and another line drawn between the shoulders. This approximation turns out to be true only when skiers don't incline very far into their turns. Now that skis allow us to make turns with high inclination angles, this rule of thumb is no longer valid.

Hip Height

A lot has been said by coaches and instructors about keeping the hips up. This is a useful teaching method that addresses the important technical issue of how high or low the skier's neutral stance is. Too high, and you'll be thrown around by changes in terrain, and if your skis suddenly slow down or speed up, you won't be able to react effectively. Too low, and you limit your range of motion to absorb bumps and place greater demands on your muscles.

There's one particular danger in the hips themselves getting too low, and this has to do with exposing the knee's anterior cruciate ligament (ACL) to possible injury. When the hips are higher than the knees, the hamstring muscles can, by contracting, provide support to each knee similar to that of the ACL. When the hips get lower than the knees, however, the hamstrings can't provide that support, and the ACL is on its own. That's why the classic ACL injury occurs not just when the skier is leaning back but when the skier's hips are low. It makes sense, then, to adopt a vertical neutral point that keeps the hips from getting below the knees, especially when skiing through compressions.

Lower-Back Posture

Much of your ability to move smoothly through the turn and terrain comes from the compliance and strength of your midbody, often called the core. Your hips and lower back must be able to flex and twist easily while stabilizing everything above them. Otherwise, your legs and upper body can't act independently, your legs can't manipulate the skis with as much facility, and the steadiness of your upper body as the counterweight that applies force to the proper spot on the skis is jeopardized.

Good midbody posture has the lower back slightly rounded and the pelvis titled neither forward nor back, as shown in figure 4.10. This is accomplished with balanced contractions of the hip flexors (primarily the iliopsoas muscles), hip extensors (gluteus maximus), abdominals, and lower-back muscles. Any feeling of unbalanced static tension in any of these is a sign that something's not right.

Two types of unbalanced static contractions in this area are common. The first is tightening the hip flexors and muscles of the lower back, making it arch and tilting the hips forward, as shown in figure 4.11. The second, and opposite, problem is a static tightening of the abdominals and buttocks (gluteus maximus), tucking the butt in and tilting the hips backward, as shown in figure 4.12. Both of these contractions lock up the midbody. There's a good chance you won't feel either of these problems if you have them, so the best way to tell if you do is by watching video of yourself shot from the side. The solution to both problems is to relax the muscles that are being statically contracted and to actively roll the hips slightly in the opposite direction to put the pelvis in its optimal neutral posture.

FIGURE 4.10 The skier's lower back should be slightly rounded, and the pelvis neutral in the sagittal plane. This avoids excessive static contractions that tie up the midbody. Skier: Carol Levine.

FIGURE 4.11 A statically arched lower back and anterior pelvic tilt: The pelvis is rotated forward in the sagittal plane.

FIGURE 4.12   **A posterior pelvic tilt: The pelvis is rotated backward in the sagittal plane.**

Steady Head

All great skiers keep their heads quiet and steady while they ski. Periodically tipping the head forward in the sagittal plane to look at the skis is a bad habit that many skiers have but few are aware of. Some might do it to check on the snow directly in front of them, some to see if their skis are close together, and some because they're afraid their skis will cross. Whatever the cause, it's a habit that's hard, but very important, to break. And while it isn't an issue of alignment in the same sense as the other topics in this chapter, it's a common issue that gets in the way of good skiing.

There are two problems with tipping the head forward. The first is that looking directly in front of you while you ski is like looking at the hood of your car while you're driving. Your attention should be focused farther in front. The second is that moving your head disturbs your sense of balance. Your head contains two of the most important components contributing to your sense of balance and orientation in space: the eyes and the inner ears. When you ski, your brain is constantly integrating the information from your eyes, inner ears, and other senses to determine your body's orientation in space and in relation to the balance axis. Moving your head around jumbles the images from your eyes as well as the information from your inner ears, making your brain's job that much harder and its assessments less accurate.

 The best way to find out if you tip your head while skiing is, again, to watch video of yourself. If you can't break the habit by consciously making yourself look ahead at all times, I know a sure-fire, though somewhat embarrassing, cure: Find an old pair of goggles and cover the lower half of the lens with duct tape. Ski with these goggles and you'll know instantly when you tip your head. Do this for a few runs a day for a week, and you'll kick the habit.

Alignment in the Frontal Plane

Viewing the skier in the frontal plane (figure 4.13) shows us things about the alignment of joints, muscles, and the center of gravity that have important effects on the skier's ability to control the skis' edges while balancing against the forces of the turn, and to control how the skier's weight is distributed between the inside and outside skis.

FIGURE 4.13   The skier viewed in the frontal plane. Skier: Jerry Berg.

Width of Stance

Until the early 1970s, it seemed that all recreational skiers wanted to ski with their feet close together. Around that time the American ski instruction community started paying more attention to what the best racers in the world were doing and realized that the aesthetic benefits of an ultranarrow stance are heavily outweighed by its functional liabilities—something racers had known for a long time. Since then there has been universal agreement that a skier's feet should be far enough apart that the legs can work independently without getting in each other's way. Otherwise, stance-width preference varies among the world's best skiers (figures 4.14 and 10.1, p. 158).

FIGURE 4.14   Rainer Schoenfelder, a top-level Austrian slalom racer, has a narrow stance for a World Cup skier, but one that is still functional because his legs can work independently. Compare his stance with that of Mario Matt in the same turns in figure 10.1 (p. 158).

FIGURE 4.15 This stance is too narrow. The legs get in each other's way, making them act as one. Leg rotation and proper angulation (important techniques discussed in chapters 7 and 8, respectively) are difficult to perform in this tight a stance, which is why the skier powers his turn with upper-body rotation (also described in chapter 7) and is not carving.

Spacing the feet about the width of the hip joints is a good starting point. Note that this is narrower than the entire pelvis. (You can see where your hip joints are by rotating your legs inward and outward, and putting your fingers on the legs' pivot points.) A stance much narrower than that will likely impede leg independence (figure 4.15). A wider stance works, too, and is more stable, but only up to a point. When the feet get too wide, the weight of the inside leg pulls the skier to the inside of the turn, compromising good lateral balance. And in a tightly carved, steeply inclined turn, there just isn't room enough to the inside of the turn for that wide a stance.

Take another look at figure 4.7 on page 61. In the normal, untilted frame, it might look as if Didier Cuche's stance is somewhat wide. When we look at the tilted frame, though, it's clear that his stance isn't wide at all. His feet are split vertically, not laterally.

Some world-class slalom and giant slalom skiers widen their stance in the transition and narrow it in the carving phase of some turns (figure 4.16). The wide stance helps the skier quickly establish inclination relative to the new outside ski, and is useful for free skiing, too. There are two reasons for narrowing the stance in the carving

FIGURE 4.16 Kathrin Zettel widens her stance in the transition and narrows it as she passes the pole. Widening her stance in the transition helps her to quickly establish inclination in the new turn (explained in chapter 9). Reducing it to hip width in the carving phase allows her to incline deeply into the turn and get close to the pole. Other examples of this can be seen in figures 4.4 (p. 58), 10.1 (p. 158), and 3.1 (p. 35).

phase: First, it helps the racer get closer to the gate. Second, as described earlier, there is a practical limitation to how wide the stance can be in a steeply inclined, tightly carved turn. This shift in stance is not a universal practice among top-level racers, however. Many maintain a fairly consistent stance width at all times.

Deep moguls favor the narrowest stance that is practical (figure 4.17). The most tractable line through a trough might not be very wide, and having the skis close together minimizes the likelihood that one of them will run into something that the other one doesn't. When we see a great skier in moguls, it's easy to get the impression that the legs are acting as one. That's not the case. Part of a great moguls skier's brilliance is the ability to ski in that narrow stance while maintaining active, and virtually invisible, independence in the legs.

FIGURE 4.17   Expert bump skiers generally use a narrow stance in deep moguls. Although it's hard to see, their legs still act independently. Skier: Jerry Berg.

Relative Alignment of Lower Legs

A neutral, home-base alignment of the lower legs, viewed from the front, has them parallel to each other. This is one of those neutral points that good skiers often pass through as they go from turn to turn but don't necessarily maintain throughout the turn. Some top-level skiers maintain a nearly parallel alignment much of the time, but many of the best skiers in the world are seen to have their outside leg tipped noticeably farther into the turn than their inside leg much of the time, as shown in figure 4.18.

Twenty years ago we often saw some of the best skiers in the world cranking their outside knee into the turn without a similar movement of the inside knee, resulting in a stance that has come to be called an A-frame. Because today's skis hold so much better in tight arcs, we carry some weight on the inside ski in many turns, and

a

b

FIGURE 4.18 Two top-flight competitors from the United States show differences in relative lower-leg alignment. Bode Miller, in 4.18*a*, rotates his outside leg farther toward the inside of the turn than his inside leg. This is typical of his skiing. Daron Rahlves on the other hand, in 4.18*b*, moves his legs more synchronously, as is his style. Rahlves and Miller, both of the United States, had nearly identical times on this run, with Miller winning the race and Rahlves placing second, just 0.3 seconds behind.

FIGURE 4.19 Lindsey Vonn, winning the 2005 U.S. National Super G Championship. She edges her new outside early in the turn to get it engaged and carving. At the same time, she uses her inside ski for support but doesn't try to make it carve.

our steering angles are much smaller. As a result, we generally ski with less outside knee angulation than we used to, and often move the inside knee into the turn to help the inside ski grip. This has reduced the difference between the lateral inclinations of the lower legs, and the A-frame is not as common or pronounced as it once was.

In recent years skiers have sometimes been told to ski with "parallel shins" or "parallel leg shafts." They're told that the lower legs, when viewed from the front, should be parallel at all times. Although this is a great exercise for developing good, active use of the inside leg, it's not something that everyone should do all the time. There are plenty of examples of indisputably great skiers who simply don't ski that way, such as Lindsey Vonn, shown in figure 4.19. Working to keep the lower legs parallel for its own sake is problematic. Doing so works against the fundamental principle of leg independence and can easily cause a skier to get blocked up and stiff in the hips, compromising independence between the upper and lower body. Skiers who work too hard at keeping their shins parallel often display several adverse effects: a stiff core, an overly square stance with no counter, and poor hip angulation (discussed later in this chapter and in chapter 8).

Torso, Hip, Knee, and Ankle Alignment

Good skiing, especially for carved turns, depends on good lateral alignment of the ankle, knee, and hip joint of each leg. The platform angle is part of the equation, too, but that aspect of alignment is a matter of boot setup and is addressed in chapter 10.

The commonly accepted neutral knee alignment for recreational skiers is defined by straight running. When you're going straight down the fall line on a gentle to moderate slope with your feet a comfortable, natural distance apart, your skis should run flat on the snow and your knees should be directly over your feet. This is a good starting point, but it begs a few questions: What is comfortable and natural? Does this work for people who are naturally bowlegged, knock-kneed, or pigeon toed? Most important, we spend most of our time turning, and that's when edge control is most critical. So should turning, rather than straight running, dictate proper lateral knee alignment?

The last question is key. When you're turning, you are balancing against a large force on an edged outside ski and against a considerably smaller force on the inside ski. Because of your inclination, your outside and inside legs are flexed differently, and your pelvis and torso are tipped outward in relation to the balance axis, as described later. This is a much different posture from what you use in a straight run.

Because the large majority of the load in carved turns is on the outside ski, that's the leg we'll focus on. In such a turn, a line drawn from the center of gravity to the inside edge of the outside ski should pass through the head of the outside femur when viewed in the frontal plane. The outside knee should also be in that line, or a bit inside of it. This is shown in figure 4.20. The ankle also must be reasonably close to the line, a subject treated in more detail in chapter 8. If the boots are canted correctly, the ski's platform angle will also be right about 90 degrees. Most misalignments of the knee here are caused by improperly canted boots (covered in chapter 10).

Proper alignment keeps the knee in a strong place while the leg flexes and extends, and balances the mass of the upper body on the head of the femur. From this alignment, the skier can turn the leg inward to increase the ski's edge and platform angles to tighten the turn or to rotate the leg outward to make the ski slip.

FIGURE 4.20 Good lateral alignment of the hip, knee, and ankle in the frontal plane in a carved turn. Skier: Jerry Berg.

Pelvis and Torso Tilt

EXERCISE

When turning, a good skier has more weight on the outside ski than the inside ski—sometimes all of it—virtually all of the time. For this to happen, the skier's balance axis must be closer to the outside foot than the inside foot. To put this in real-world terms, stand in front of a full-length mirror, balance on your right foot, and watch yourself as you touch the outside of your right knee with your right hand (see figure 8.6*a* on p. 127). What you've done is moved your balance axis closer to that foot. To accomplish this, you tilted your pelvis and torso in the frontal plane until your center of gravity was balanced over the head of your femur. If you look carefully in the mirror, you'll see that your shoulders are tilted more than your hips. The tilt of your hips is a rotation in the frontal plane of the pelvis itself on the head of the femur, and the tilt of your shoulders is the result of small rotations in each of the vertebrae of your spine.

FIGURE 4.21 Jean-Baptiste Grange, a preeminent World Cup slalom skier for France and winner of the World Cup slalom title in 2009, gets his balance axis over the outside ski mostly by titling his pelvis and torso in the frontal plane.

Good skiers get most or all of their weight on the outside ski through a combination of what you just did in front of the mirror and countering, which is discussed later in this chapter (see Alignment in the Transverse Plane, p. 73). Together, these movements constitute *hip angulation,* which is further detailed in chapter 8. The best skiers in the world vary in how much they tilt in the frontal plane and how much they counter, but they all do some of each (figures 4.21 and 8.7, p. 128).

Coaches and instructors have talked for decades about the importance of the hips and shoulders being "level," referring to the alignment of an imaginary line passing through the heads of the femurs and another through the shoulders. When athletes were inclining 30 or 40 degrees into a turn, those lines were approximately level with respect to the snow. That is, the lines were approximately perpendicular to gravity. With current angles of inclination we can see that the hips and shoulders of the world's best skiers are seldom truly level. The important aspect of hip and shoulder alignment in the frontal plane is not how they line up in relation to the snow or to gravity, but how they line up relative to the balance axis: They need to be tipped toward the outside relative to that line. But emphasizing the importance of the hips and shoulders being "level" was, and still is, a good coaching method. What feels level to a skier generally turns out to be a good alignment, whether it is literally level or not.

Attaining good hip alignment starts with an awareness of where the inside hip is during the turn's initiation phase. You develop that awareness by making lots and lots of turns while focusing on just that, starting in simplified environments—smooth snow, moderate pitch, and no distractions—and progressing to more complex situations. If your inside hip drops going into the turn, a common problem, your center of gravity will almost certainly fall toward the inside of the turn, and you won't enter the control phase with the right amount of hip angulation. As a result, you'll skid and slip. A good exercise to help you keep your hips aligned properly is shown in figure 4.22. At the very start of the turn, put your outside hand on your hip, and reach up and forward with your inside hand. Keep reaching up and forward with the inside hand all the way through a medium-sized round, clean turn, then switch hands as you go into the next.

Tilting the shoulders into the turn, or simply not tilting the torso sufficiently outward relative to the balance axis, is one of the most common problems in skiing, and it's easy to spot. Developing good shoulder alignment starts with the hands, and exercises that emphasize keeping the hands "level," in the sense that a line between them is tilted outward with respect to the balance axis, usually produce good results. Looping a piece of string around the hands, as described in chapter 9 (see figure 9.8, p. 143), is one good exercise. Another is skiing with the poles held crosswise in front of you, as shown in figure 4.23.

EXERCISE

FIGURE 4.22 This simple exercise will help you become aware of what it feels like to keep your hips "level." The turns you make should be complete, round arcs. Skier: Carol Levine.

EXERCISE

FIGURE 4.23 This classic exercise, skiing while holding your poles in front of you, level with the snow, helps develop good arm and shoulder alignment in the frontal plane. Skier: David N. Oliver.

FIGURE 4.24 This skier tilts his head into the turn, which pulls his whole upper body in that direction. His hip moves to the outside to compensate, reducing his hip angulation and requiring him to use excessive knee angulation.

Tipping your head to one side or the other while you ski has an effect on your balance similar to that of tilting your head forward to look at your ski tips (discussed earlier in the chapter). In addition to affecting your balance, tipping your head to the side almost always causes the rest of your body to follow suit, which is especially bad if you tip it to the inside of the turn (figure 4.24). Skiers who do this bank chronically to the inside of their turns and have too little hip angulation. On the other hand, many excellent skiers often tip their heads a bit to the outside of the turn to increase hip angulation and get their balance more over the outside ski (figure 4.25).

FIGURE 4.25 Benjamin Raich tips his head outward slightly in these particular turns, helping the alignment of his torso and hips in the frontal plane. Note that this is a small adjustment and shouldn't be overdone.

Alignment in the Transverse Plane

We don't often view skiers in the transverse plane—from directly above (figure 4.26)—but one of the most subtle and important facets of body alignment appears from this vantage: counter. Too much or too little of this stance element can compromise all the good movements you make. Just how you should arrange your body in this plane depends on many aspects of your particular body type, so alignment in this regard varies widely among the best of skiers.

Viewed in the transverse plane, a good skier's pelvis and torso won't generally face exactly in the direction the skis are pointing when the skier is in a turn. Instead they'll be rotated about the balance axis toward the outside of the turn (figure 4.27). This alignment is called *counter*, and the movement of turning the hips and torso in that direction is called *countering*. (Don't confuse these terms with *counterrotation*, described in chapter 7. They're all standard terms in ski teaching and coaching, and unfortunately sound very similar. Counter and countering are very close in meaning, but counterrotation refers to a much different concept.) Counter helps the skier move the balance axis toward the outside ski (as described on page 70) without tilting the pelvis and torso excessively in the frontal plane. By first countering, the skier can move the balance axis toward the outside ski by bending forward at the waist in the sagittal plane, instead of just tilting the hips and torso sideways in the frontal plane. Both the pelvis and spine have limited flexibility in that direction, and stiffen up quickly when bent very far that way. Countering also shifts much of the load of supporting the upper body, which can be considerable, from weak muscles to stronger ones.

FIGURE 4.26   The skier viewed in the transverse plane. Skier: Jerry Berg.

FIGURE 4.27   Hermann Maier counters by turning his hips and shoulders slightly toward the outside of the turn.

The strongest muscles can support the greatest loads with the most finesse. Ask a muscle to work against a load that taxes its limits, and it can't work with precision. The biggest, strongest muscles in your body are those of the thigh and buttocks. So when you're balancing against big forces in a turn, these are the muscles you want to have supporting and balancing your upper body. The closer the balance axis gets to the outside foot, the more the hips and torso need to counter to line up the load with those muscles of the outside leg. Most countering takes place in the ball-and-socket joint where the femur meets the pelvis. A smaller amount also occurs throughout the spinal column, so that the shoulders are countered slightly more than the hips.

Figure 4.28 shows a good combination of lateral tilt and countering in a turn with a lot of force. In some turns, especially those of medium radius and larger, you should establish counter by the end of the transition so your body is well aligned to balance against the force that you'll encounter in the control phase (see figures 8.9, p. 130, and 9.9, p. 144). In other turns, such as short radius turns on steep slopes, the big force doesn't come until after the fall line (see figures 8.8, p. 129, and 14.4, p. 203), and your upper body won't turn toward the outside so much as your legs will turn under your body to put you in a countered stance. Look at the inset frames in figures 8.8 and 14.4 and imagine how contorted the skiers would be if they were still balanced over the downhill ski but their upper bodies weren't countered—that is, if their torsos were facing the camera. Figure 4.29 shows a skier doing just that.

Because proper counter brings into play the best muscles for balancing against the force of the turn, you get the feeling of being supported by your bones, especially in medium to large radius turns. A less-than-optimal alignment, which enlists weaker muscles to the task, makes you feel like your muscles are doing more work.

FIGURE 4.28 Ted Ligety pulls something in the neighborhood of 3Gs at the bottom of this giant slalom turn, balanced entirely on his outside ski. The head of his outside femur and his outside knee are in a line in the frontal plane with his center of gravity and the edge of his ski, putting him in a strong posture. He relies mostly on hip angulation to maintain the platform angle that makes his ski hold and uses knee angulation to make fine adjustments to the ski's edge and platform angle. The hip angulation is produced by a well-coordinated combination of lateral tilt of the pelvis and spine, countering, and flexing forward at the hips and lower back. Much more knee angulation than this would not allow his leg to flex and extend smoothly and could be unsafe for his knee under this much load.

Besides being big, strong muscles, the thigh and buttocks are also the principle muscles used to control the overall flexion and extension of the body along the balance axis. So when you're properly countered, you can move up and down smoothly through terrain and the phases of turns while maintaining hip angulation.

A good way to tell if your degree of counter is in the ballpark is to increase and decrease it while making medium radius turns. Search for the point at which you feel that you're being supported by your bones rather than your muscles. This means that you've aligned your hip so that you're balancing against the force on your upper body with your

FIGURE 4.29   Hip angulation without countering. Weak muscles are used to tilt the torso to the outside. The skier is very stiff and will not be able to move smoothly through terrain variations.

thigh and buttock muscles. Because hip angulation and countering aren't second nature for most skiers, you should also do some exercises to develop your range of hip angulation and countering.

EXERCISE

Have a friend pull on your poles, as shown in figure 4.30. This gives you the feeling of hip angulation and countering. Pointing your uphill ski down the hill turns your hip over the femur, and reaching with your arms makes you fold at the waist—both essential elements of hip angulation. This exercise pulls you into an exaggerated posture to give you the feeling of what it means to turn your hip on top of your femur and lean your upper body out over your outside ski.

a

b

FIGURE 4.30   (a) This exercise helps the skier angulate at the hip and counter; (b) pointing the uphill ski down the hill increases the skier's counter. As a bonus, this exercise allows the skier to experience what it feels like to have the inside hand even with the outside hand, have weight focused on the outside ski, and make the ski hold. Skiers: Andy Gould and Cait Boyd.

Gender Differences in Countering and Hip Angulation

The distribution of mass in women's bodies is, in general, different from that of men. Women carry proportionately more mass in and around the hips and less in their upper torsos. How far into a turn a skier should put the hips depends on the location of the outside hip joint and the location of the ankle with respect to the balance axis. How far to the outside a skier must put the shoulders, on the other hand, is dictated by how much weight that aforementioned hip movement puts to the inside of the turn. In other words, the upper body is put to the outside of the turn to counterbalance the movement of the hip to the inside. And because most women's hips have relatively more mass than men's, and their shoulders less, women must usually counter and angulate at the hips more than men to stay in balance while getting the same edge control.

Another good exercise for developing hip angulation and countering is the javelin turn, demonstrated in figure 4.31. The idea is simple: Make a turn and, when you get to the fall line, pick your inside ski up and point its tip toward the outside of the turn. As the turn progresses, point the ski more and more toward the outside. The more you can cross it over the outside ski, the better. This turns your hip to a countered position and puts it to the inside of the turn. Really good skiers can make javelin turns of just about any size on just about any terrain. This exercise dates back to the mid-1960s, when Art Furrer, a Swiss who was probably the first well-known trick skier, invented the maneuver for his repertoire. He named the move after the model of ski that his supplier, Hart, was promoting at the time.

FIGURE 4.31   A javelin turn. Picking the inside ski up and pointing it toward the outside of the turn makes the skier's hip turn toward the outside, putting him in a countered stance. Skier: Brian Blackstock.

CHAPTER 5

Fore and Aft

Skiers move forward (fore) and backward (aft) in relation to their skis primarily to maintain stability. The first skill beginners learn when making their initial straight runs on those slippery boards is how to keep up with their feet as their skis accelerate, and how to keep upright as their skis slow to a stop. Viewed from the side, in the sagittal plane, the skier is challenged with keeping the balance axis going through the feet. As a skier gains experience and progresses to fresh challenges, variations in terrain and the character of the snow place similar demands on balance and require similar adjustments from the skier (figure 5.1). Moguls, variable loose snow, and some of the most entertaining natural features of a ski slope all require constant fore–aft adjustments (figure 5.2).

At a finer level of control than is required just to stay in balance, fore and aft movements enable skiers to manipulate the ski's turning behavior: its self-steering effect, described in chapter 2. They do this by shifting the distribution of pressure along the ski's length, which controls the ski's tendency to oversteer and determines whether one part of the ski bends into more reverse camber than another.

FIGURE 5.1   The most basic balancing movements a skier makes are fore–aft movements that control the relative position of the center of gravity and the feet in the sagittal plane, as this skier does when he moves his feet forward of his center of gravity in anticipation of landing against a bump. Skier: Brian Blackstock.

FIGURE 5.2   Moguls require the skier to move fore and aft in anticipation of the terrain. Dropping over a bump into the trough, the skier presses forward to avoid being left on his heels. Approaching the end of the trough, he prepares to ski into the next mogul by pushing his feet ahead. Skier: Jerry Berg.

Moving Fore and Aft

Ask most skiers to move from tip to tail on their skis, and they'll lean their whole bodies to and fro (figure 5.3). This is how they've learned to control fore–aft balance over a lifetime of standing on surfaces that give them reliable and significant friction. They move their centers of gravity back and forth over their feet, which don't move.

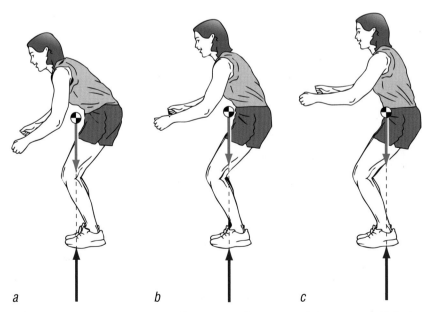

a   *b*   *c*

FIGURE 5.3   In most nonskiing situations, people adjust their fore–aft balance by moving their upper bodies back and forth over their feet.

When standing on something slippery, like skis on snow, there's a better way to make most fore–aft adjustments: by sliding your feet back and forth under your body (figures 5.4 and 5.5). Because your skis, boots, bindings, and lower legs are much less massive than your torso, arms, and head, you can adjust more quickly and precisely this way than by moving your upper body. The primary action happens in the ankles, with a bit of movement at the knee.

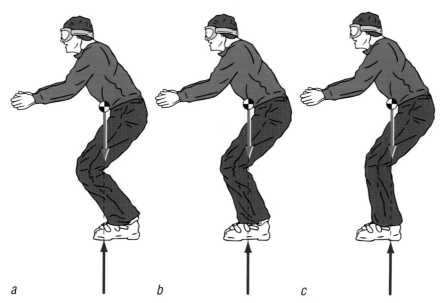

a   *b*   *c*

FIGURE 5.4   The expert skier controls pressure on the skis fore and aft by moving the feet forward and backward under the body. This is done primarily by flexing and straightening the ankles.

FIGURE 5.5   2007 World Cup overall champion Nicole Hosp of Austria bends her ankles to move her balance forward as she enters this turn. In the last two frames, she progressively straightens her ankles, moving her feet forward relative to her center of gravity.

Bode Miller

Bode Miller is one of the best and most innovative skiers of his time. Bode finished in the top four in the race for the overall World Cup for seven straight years, from 2002 to 2008. He has won more World Cup races than any other American. He is also one of only two men—the other being Marc Girardelli—to have won World Cup races in all five disciplines in a single season. While it took Girardelli most of the season to accomplish this feat, Miller did it in six weeks.

While a teenager, Miller realized before anyone else the potential of shaped skis for racing, choosing to compete on recreational shaped skis when they first appeared on the market rather than the best racing skis of the time, which had conventional sidecuts. And he won races on them. As he moved to international competition and began his rise to the highest ranks, coaches and competitors could see that it was only a matter of time before he would be the man to beat in slalom and giant slalom.

Bode did become that man. It was as if he saw the possibilities in slalom and giant slalom technique and line, and was waiting for the equipment to catch up with him. As it did, and as his technique and tactics developed, he became not just the man to beat, but the man to watch. He consistently tested the limits of early inclination and edge angle, using aggressive knee angulation to get the ski engaged and carving. This enabled him to push his line to the absolute limit. When he pushed it too hard, his innate athleticism and ability to improvise usually kept him in the course.

In the 2004-05 season, Miller turned his attention to downhill and super G, and won the overall World Cup title. In addition, he won the super G crown and was second for the season in both giant slalom and downhill. He has continued to be successful in speed events, as many of the great skiers before him—such as Girardelli, Aamodt, and Kjus—were in the latter halves of their careers.

Bode has left an indelible mark on skiing and ski racing. He envisioned what was possible and went for it, daring everyone else to match him. Time and again he has proven that his vision was true, and that few were capable of matching it.

Straightening the ankle, or plantarflexion, pushes the foot forward. Bending the ankle, or dorsiflexion, pulls the foot back. To feel these movements, start from a flexed stance that places your center of gravity over the arches of your feet, with your ankles bent slightly so your shins are lightly touching the tongues of your boots. To shift your balance forward from this neutral position, dorsiflex by pushing your knees forward, drawing your feet back, or pulling your toes up. (These are all essentially the same movement.) As your shins start to press firmly against the tongues of your boots, the boots act like levers to increase the shift in pressure toward the tips of your skis. To move your balance back, straighten your ankles, or plantarflex them. You can think of sliding your feet forward, or pushing your toes down. Move only your feet. Whatever you do, don't rock your upper body backward. Once your calf muscles have started to press against the backs of your boots, the pressure will shift quickly toward the tails of your skis.

EXERCISE

The key is to control the pressure as much as possible by bending and straightening the ankles only (see figure 5.7, p. 82). Of all the joints in your body, the ankles have the greatest effect on your fore–aft balance. Changing the flex in the ankles by 10 degrees, for example, moves an average person's center of gravity forward by about 6 inches (15 cm), about the span from the ball of the foot to the heel. Once your knees, hips, and shoulders are comfortably flexed in an athletic posture, they should have minimal involvement in fore–aft adjustments.

Making turns in a tuck on a flat run or road, as shown in figure 5.6, is a good exercise for developing fore–aft movement in the ankles. As you go into the turn, move forward over your skis by bending your ankles, feeling an increase in pressure under the balls of your feet and against the tongues of your boots. As you finish the turn, slide your feet forward until you feel light pressure from your boot cuffs on the backs of your legs. Keep your chest down and your back flat. This will prevent you from moving your center of gravity by flexing or extending at the waist or dropping your hips.

EXERCISE

FIGURE 5.6 Turning in a tuck is a good exercise for many skiing skills, including fore and aft movements using the ankles. Here the skier flexes his ankles through the carving phase of the turn, then straightens them coming out of the turn by sliding his feet forward. The tuck position isolates the upper body, preventing the skier from making movements above the hips that should be done with the legs. Skier: David N. Oliver.

As you make these movements, you should be able to feel the spot under your feet where the pressure is highest. This is the point your center of gravity is directly over, as determined by the balance axis: the line of action of gravity and centrifugal force combined.

Your ski boots aren't shoes. They are your skis' handles, and just as you manipulate a tennis racket or golf club through its handle, you manipulate your skis with your boots. The higher and stiffer they are, the more responsive your skis will be to small movements of your legs and ankles. Pressing sharply against the front of the boot puts a shot of pressure on the ski's forebody. Unless this pressure is accompanied by a movement of your center of gravity toward the tip of the ski, it will be short lived. The back of the boot provides leverage on the tail of the ski and support that enables you to pressure the tail quickly without getting out of balance (figure 5.7).

FIGURE 5.7   Pushing against the front or back of the boot cuff causes big shifts in the distribution of pressure fore and aft along the ski. Lindsey Vonn gets strong tip pressure by flexing the front of her boot, and then quickly moves that pressure to the tail by straightening her ankle and pushing on the back of the boot.

Because boots are so critical, take care when selecting a pair, considering the type of skiing you do the most. To ski in the stiffest boots requires great finesse and ability, and you should be especially careful not to buy boots that are too stiff in the front. You'll ski better in a boot that's a bit too soft than one that's too stiff. See chapter 10 for more information on boots.

Finding the Skis' Neutral Point

Every pair of skis has an optimal fore and aft neutral spot that's dictated by a combination of design factors. Skis designed primarily for medium radius turns (giant slalom skis, for example) tend to favor a neutral point at or just behind the ball of the foot, whereas skis designed for short radius turns (such as slalom skis) tend to favor a stance just a bit farther back than that. More forgiving skis have a wider range over which they respond well, whereas more demanding skis have a narrower range.

The following exercise, which instructors call pivot slips, is a good way to find a pair of skis' neutral point. Shown in figure 5.8, pivot slips are also a useful warm-up exercise and a good way to get acquainted with a new pair of skis or boots. I suggest making them the first thing you do when you demo a pair of skis. Start off down the fall line on a gentle slope or road. Once underway, swivel your skis back and forth 180 degrees, flat on the snow, without your body's path deviating from the fall line. Use your feet and knees to turn the skis, keeping them flat on the snow. The skis should brush lightly against the snow, but not grip or catch. You'll likely need to adjust both up and down and fore and aft to find just the right stance. Every pair of boots requires a slightly different amount of bend at the ankles, knees, and waist, and every pair of skis has its own neutral point fore and aft.

FIGURE 5.8   Pivot slips. The skis pivot back and forth while the skier's center of gravity continues in a straight line. This exercise teaches the skier where the skis' neutral pivot point is, fore and aft. Skier: Andy Gould.

Fore–Aft Balance

Because skis are so slippery fore and aft, balancing on them in the sagittal plane is much different than most other situations. You're in balance fore and aft when the balance axis, not the line of gravity, goes through your feet (figures 1.8, p. 9, and 4.3, p. 57). This is illustrated by the difference in the way beginners and experienced skiers get off a chair lift that has an unloading ramp they must ski down.

Most people taking up skiing are unaccustomed to standing on things as slippery as skis. Their bodies have learned to balance against the considerable friction that's been under their feet all their lives, and this is why so many beginners fall over the first time they get off a chair lift. Seeing that they are about to stand up on a slope (the unloading ramp), they assume a stance that anticipates a friction force pushing back up the slope on them. When that friction fails to materialize, they're left off balance.

The beginning skier's expectation is shown in figure 5.9*a*; the reality is shown in figures 5.9*b* and 5.9*c*. For this person on a slope, the force that gravity exerts on her can be resolved into two components: G_n, which is perpendicular to the bottom of her skis and is therefore aligned with her balance axis, and G_s, which is trying to make her slide down the hill. In figure *a*, the surface on which she's standing can counterbalance both those components. Because the surface is firm, it exerts S_n on her, and because there is friction between it and her shoes, it exerts S_f on her. On skis, depicted in figures *b* and *c*, things are different. S_f is, for all intents and purposes, gone, and S can only oppose G_n. Because G_s is unopposed, it accelerates the skier down the hill. In figure *b*, the skier is in the same stance relative to her feet that she was in figure *a*. If the skier could hold herself in a position with her balance axis behind her feet, using the tail for support, she might not fall over, but the human body isn't built in a way that makes this possible. Consequently, the force from the snow, S, stays under her feet and is not aligned with the force it is opposing, G_n. A torque is exerted on the skier, and she falls over backward. In figure *c*, the skier has aligned the force from the snow and G_n, her balance axis, and although she still accelerates down the hill, she's stable.

a *b* *c*

FIGURE 5.9 Beginning skiers often fall over backward when they get off a chair lift because they don't compensate for the absence of friction. The balance axis, which is aligned here with G_n, is always perpendicular to the bottom of the skis and must pass through the feet.

The important point is this: The skier's fore and aft balance point has little to do with the slope of the hill because the hill is slippery. To be in balance, the skier must move the body forward relative to the feet when the slope gets steeper.

Because alpine boots are fixed so solidly to the skis, the skier's base of support is somewhat expanded forward and back. The skier can recover from lurching forward or sitting back in a way that would otherwise be impossible. Telemark skiers, with free-heel equipment, don't have that luxury, but do have the ability to adjust the length of their base of support (figure 5.10). The Telemark stance is functional, not stylistic, and the best Telemark skiers don't exaggerate it. They split their feet only as much as they need to manage their fore and aft balance in the situation at hand.

FIGURE 5.10   Telemark turns give the free-heel skier stability fore and aft. The split of the feet provides a base of support whose length fore and aft is adjustable, potentially much bigger than that of an alpine ski boot in a fixed-heel binding. This is especially useful in the inconsistent snow conditions found in the back country. Skier: Patti Banks.

Synchronizing Fore and Aft Movements With Phases of the Turn

When the skier's center of gravity moves forward and backward over the skis, the distribution of pressure along their length changes too. If the skis are edged and turning, the change in that distribution of pressure can have a marked effect on the skis' self-steering behavior, as described in chapter 2. Shifting pressure forward increases their self-steering effect, making the turn tighter. Shifting pressure toward the tail reduces the effect if the ski is edged, broadening the turn.

We want to begin the control phase of most turns with at least a bit of extra tip pressure, because this makes the ski turn more sharply. In the completion phase, on the other hand, we generally want the ski to stop turning, so we shift pressure back to the middle or even to the tail of the ski. This is the typical flow of fore–aft pressure in turns (figure 5.11). In terms of where the balance axis goes through your feet, the range of movement in free skiing is usually small (perhaps an inch or two, and rarely more than from the ball of the foot to the back of the arch), but in aggressive turns the range might be larger.

FIGURE 5.11   In most turns balance should flow from forward to back through the control phase. The range of movement of the fore and aft balance point for free skiing is usually small (less than a couple of inches, and rarely more than from the ball of the foot to the back of the arch), but in aggressive turns the range might be bigger. Skier: David N. Oliver.

I've just made two statements that might appear to be at odds with each other. First, I said that you want to enter the control phase of the turn with pressure on the forebody of the ski. Then I said you want to finish the turn farther back on the ski. Because the end of one turn often melds seamlessly with the start of the next, wouldn't the finish of one turn leave you in the wrong place on the ski (back) as you enter the next turn? Not necessarily. In the transition, your center of gravity travels a shorter path between turns than your feet (see figure 9.10, p. 145). Then during this initiation phase, the skis are turned to their initial steering angle. This puts your center of gravity farther forward over the ski than it was at the end of the preceding turn. Just how far forward your center of gravity will be is determined by the angle of its trajectory to the path of your feet, your initial steering angle in your new turn, and how much you draw your feet back going into the turn (figures 5.12 and 11.4, p. 183).

Only on smooth slopes and consistent snow do these cyclic fore and aft movements happen in isolation. In the real world of skiing, the arcs of your turns are folded over bumps, bent through dips, and banked off counterslopes, all of which demand fore–aft adjustments. The ability to combine these movements seamlessly is one thing that separates the best skiers from the rest. If they don't look as if they're making big movements, it's because they're making them with their feet.

FIGURE 5.12 Because Ivica Kostelic's upper body travels a shorter line than his feet, he's balanced forward at the beginning of the control phase in each of these turns, even though he appears to be a bit back in the initiation.

Up and Down

Moving up and down in concert with the snow and the dynamics of the turn is a mark of a fine skier. That doesn't necessarily mean moving your center of gravity up and down, but rather extending and flexing your entire body in that direction. In fact, a good skier makes many of these movements to moderate the effects of terrain and the forces of the turn, preventing those effects and forces from causing the skier's center of gravity to move up and down. Extending the range of motion and precision of your up-and-down movements is one of the simplest and biggest steps you can take toward becoming a better skier yourself. The more range you have, the wider variety of terrain and skiing situations you'll be able to deal with. And the more precision you have in these movements, the better you'll be able to flow through those situations without your balance being disturbed. You'll be able to control the force and pressure exerted by the snow on you and your skis so they will produce the exact effects you want—running smoothly through bumps and dips, setting your edges firmly and cleanly, and jumping gaps between moguls to make airplane turns—while you stay centered over your skis.

What Do Up, Down, and Vertical Mean?

The words up, down, and vertical are so basic to our vocabularies that we assume they mean the same things to all people. But what do *up, down,* and *vertical* really mean in your frame of reference as a skier, as discussed in chapter 1? Assuming you're in balance, *up* is the direction your supporting surface pushes on you. *Down,* obviously, is the other direction: the direction in which you push on that surface. And *vertical* is the line that up and down share. In terms of the skier's frame of reference, vertical is the balance axis.

When you're standing still at the side of a ski trail, up, down, and vertical are defined only by gravity: For you, up is the direction the trees point. When you're skiing, however, you sense a different up and down, set within your own personal frame of reference. As you ski through terrain variations and turns, more forces come into play, and the balance axis isn't usually parallel with the trees, as shown in figure 6.1. Whenever the terms up, down, and vertical appear in this book, we'll be using them from the skier's frame of reference. It's the best thing you have to go by when you're skiing, and it defines the category of fundamental movements we address in this chapter.

FIGURE 6.1 A skier's sense of up and down is determined by the balance axis. This is the line along which the force from the snow on the skier acts when the skier is in balance. It defines up, down, and vertical to the skier's senses, and it's what we mean by those terms in this book. That line is always perpendicular to the bottom of the ski, so its direction changes as this skier goes up the bank. As he turns, centrifugal force tips the line toward the inside of the turn. Skier: Dave Holdcraft.

Why Move Up and Down?

Skiers move up and down to control the magnitude of the force exerted on them by the snow. The total amount of force acting between you and the snow determines how much of an effect the snow has on your motion. If you have just passed over a bump and your skis are light, you won't be able to turn or slow down because the snow can't push on you. You'll be able to pivot your skis easily, on the other hand, for the same reason.

At any point in a turn, traverse, or straight run, you want the snow to exert a particular amount of force on you. Sometimes you want a lot, and sometimes you want a little, depending on the particular place you are at in the turn you're making. If you don't move up and down at all, the contour of the snow and the virtual bump, described in chapter 3, will combine to exert changing forces on you throughout the turn that often won't be optimal for what you want to do. By extending or flexing, you augment or reduce these forces to produce the amount of overall force you want.

When going straight down the hill, you're usually interested in keeping the total force from the snow constant. If there are bumps in your path, you flex and extend to negate their effects, keeping your center of gravity moving in something close to a straight line when viewed in the sagittal plane, as Donna Weinbrecht does in figure 6.2. When making short turns through big moguls, you usually flex at the end of the turn to reduce the upward force the mogul would otherwise exert on you. Once having crossed the crest of the bump, you extend to maintain some ski–snow pressure. The larger the bumps, the more amplitude and precision you need. In both situations, you move up and down in synch with the snow to keep your center of gravity from being displaced up and down.

FIGURE 6.2   Donna Weinbrecht, formerly of the U.S. Ski Team, flexes and extends through moguls to minimize the changes in force on her center of gravity along the balance axis. She also moves her feet forward slightly as she skis into the bump, and pulls them back slightly as she passes over the crest to maintain her fore–aft balance. She has described the combination of these movements as feeling like pedaling a bicycle backward. One of the best competitive mogul skiers of all time, Weinbrecht won 5 overall World Cup titles, the first Olympic gold medal awarded in the discipline, 2 World Championship medals, and 46 World Cup victories.

Beginning skiers make movements that create only small changes in ski-snow pressure. They ski in simplified environments where only small pressure changes are created by the terrain, and they make turns that generate only small forces and no discernable virtual bump. As they progress through intermediate ability stages, skiers keep the environment simple but learn to deliberately change pressure from ski to ski, modulate the overall pressure on their skis, and make turns that generate greater forces.

By the time skiers have reached an advanced level, they have learned to make many movements to deal with anticipated and potentially disruptive pressure changes caused by terrain and the dynamics of the turn. It's fair to say that good skiers make more movements to prevent or reduce changes in the force from the snow than they make to create them.

Accounting for the Virtual Bump

Intermediates first feel the virtual bump, described in chapter 3, when they start to complete turns with significant pressure and link them together. They quickly learn to like the lift and bounce they get when they merge the completion of one turn with the initiation of the next in a seamless transition. At this point, they learn to time their own up and down movements to coincide with the ups and downs of the virtual bump. Their up movements and the rise of the virtual bump complement each other, making it easier to initiate the turn.

This synergy works well up to a point. But once you start linking tightly carved turns, you have to be prepared for virtual bumps that might launch you off the snow if you extend at the end of the turn. To maintain contact with the snow in these circumstances, you have to time your flexions and extensions as if your were skiing through bumps: You flex in the completion phase of one turn and don't extend until you start to turn down into the fall line in the next (figures 6.3 and 6.4).

a

b

FIGURE 6.3 The skier in figure *a* flexes in the transition between two tightly carved, medium radius turns. Her center of gravity is barely lifted by the virtual bump. The skier in figure *b* neither extends nor flexes in the transition and is consequently launched off the snow by the virtual bump. Skiers: *(a)* Carol Levine; *(b)* Andy Gould.

FIGURE 6.4 To moderate the effect of the virtual bump and maintain ski–snow contact, Thomas Grandi of Canada flexes through the transitions and extends into the control phases of these turns.

Uncoupling Up and Down From Fore and Aft

We move up and down on skis for different reasons than we move fore and aft. Up and down movements regulate the total amount of force the snow exerts on us, whereas fore and aft movements control the skis' behavior in response to that force and help us maintain balance. Yet most skiers can't move independently in these two directions. They have deep-rooted couplings between their vertical and fore–aft movements. Some move forward with every downward flexion and backward with every upward extension. Every possible combination of entrenched patterns can be seen out on the mountain.

To ski with real versatility, you must be able to control independently these two interactions with the snow. You need to control overall force through long vertical movements without disturbing its distribution fore and aft. Likewise, you have to move forward or backward while keeping the total force against the snow constant. See figure 6.5.

Nothing demonstrates this particular ability better than making large turns through moguls, as shown in figure 6.6, because it requires a skier to move up and down several times in a single turn while independently controlling fore–aft and lateral balance. It's as good a test as any to separate the best skiers from the rest.

a   *b*

FIGURE 6.5   Moving purely up and down versus moving purely fore and aft.

FIGURE 6.6   Making good medium to long radius turns in a field of moguls requires skiers to conform with the shape of the snow by moving up and down through a long range without affecting their fore–aft or lateral balance. Doing this well is the mark of an excellent skier. Skier: Rob Mahan.

If you can isolate the vertical movement of your center of gravity, you can control the overall force on it and the force's fore–aft distribution independently. Your body is composed of segments that pivot around joints, however, and articulating at any single joint moves your center of gravity in an arc. Consider the piston in figure 6.7. It's driven by links that move in circular arcs around pivot points, like your center of gravity is driven by your skeleton. Your task as a skier is to coordinate those rotary movements so that, like the piston, your center of gravity moves straight up and down.

The major joints we have to work with for moving vertically and fore and aft are the ankles, knees, hips, lower back, and shoulders. None of these joints, by itself, moves your center of gravity purely up and down or forward and backward. Rather, each joint moves your center of gravity in an arc. As we saw in chapter 5, the ankles are useful for making fore–aft adjustments, but as figure 6.8 shows, they have little effect on your center of gravity's vertical position. So the knees, hips, lower back, and shoulders must work together like the links driving the piston to move your center of gravity straight up and down (figure 6.9).

FIGURE 6.7 A piston moves in a straight line through coordinated rotary movements around joints, similar to the major joints in the skier's body.

FIGURE 6.8 Flexing or extending in the sagittal plane at any one of the major joints moves the skier's center of gravity in an arc within that plane. When articulations are properly combined, the skier's center of gravity moves straight up and down along the balance axis.

FIGURE 6.9 The roll between these two gates requires Lindsey Vonn to go through a long range of vertical flexion and extension to stay on the snow and get early edge pressure to make the second turn. She simultaneously makes fore–aft adjustments, first moving from being slightly forward to being in the middle of the skis in the transition, then being forward again at the start of the second turn's control phase. Note that she achieves a very low stance without bending her ankles or keeping her hips over her feet.

tip Here, then, is a good rule of thumb for uncoupling up and down movements of the center of gravity from those that move it fore and aft. Use your knees, hips, and shoulders for up and down, and use your ankles for fore and aft. As with all rules of thumb, it's a bit simplistic, but nonetheless is a good place to start. In the next section we'll look at combining articulations at the knees, hips, and shoulders to produce pure vertical motion.

Learning to Move Straight Up and Down

Everyone can move straight up and down when they're wearing sneakers. But put them in ski boots, and it's a different story. That's because ski boots, unlike sneakers, are designed to restrict ankle movement. When you're not wearing ski boots, you can move up and down using coordinated movements at the ankles, knees, hips, and lower back that your body has learned from years of experience. When you put on ski boots and step into your skis, you lose the free use of your ankles. Try to bend your ankle, and the boot stops you. Try harder, and it puts leverage on the ski's forebody, shifting pressure forward. Straighten the ankle past a certain point, and the back of the boot shifts pressure toward the tail. Try to flex using the same combination of articulations as you would in street shoes, and you'll wind up on your heels.

To move straight up and down in ski boots to accurately control the overall force from the snow, you must flex and extend with very little ankle movement. You use a different combination of articulations at the knees, hips, lower back, and shoulders than you use when you're wearing sneakers. But finding the right combination can be tricky. Bend too little at the waist, and your center of gravity moves down and back (figure 6.10*a*). Bend too much at the waist for the amount of bend at your knees, and your center of gravity moves down and forward (figure 6.10*c*). Drop your arms straight down while flexing, and your center of gravity moves back. Straighten too fast at the waist for the amount of straightening at the knees, and your center of gravity moves up and back (figure 6.10*d*). And so on.

The combination of articulations that work for you are specific to your body, depending on the length and weight of your lower legs, upper legs, hips, torso, and arms. Other important factors are your ski boots, because of their forward lean, and your bindings, which can affect the forward lean of your boots. (Forward lean is discussed in chapter 10.) The expert skier's body has learned the right articulations by making hundreds of thousands of turns. Your body can learn them that way, too, but there's no guarantee it will unless you train it properly.

EXERCISE A good way to tell if you can move straight up and down without moving fore and aft is to do check wedeln (also called hop turns; figure 6.11, p. 96). The objective is to make turns by quickly and cleanly hopping from edgeset to edgeset. Any movement of your center of gravity in the wrong direction will slow your rhythm and throw off your balance. You should be able to make at least 10 such turns in a row.

a

b

c

d

FIGURE 6.10   Each of these skiers has a different common problem with the relative articulations at major joints that makes the skier's center of gravity move fore and aft as it moves up and down: *(a)* This skier starts off centered over her feet, but as she moves down, her center of gravity moves back. To compensate for the movement of her hips toward the tails of her skis, she needs to bend forward more at the waist as she flexes. *(b-c)* Moving down and forward is another common problem. The skier in figure *b* bends his ankles as he flexes, moving his center of gravity forward and also levering on the tip of his ski with his boot. The skier in figure *c* goes forward as he flexes because all his flexion is at the waist. He needs to bend his knees at the same time. *(d)* Another common vertical-motion problem is moving up and back.

FIGURE 6.11 Check wedeln, or hop turns, is a great exercise for developing clean up and down movements. Try to crisply link 10 or more in a row—the quicker the better. If you're moving straight up and down, your skis will be parallel to the snow. Skier: Rick Rauch.

EXERCISE To train your body to move straight up and down, start by practicing on a hard, level floor with your boots buckled tightly. Move up and down through as long a range as possible, paying close attention to your fore–aft balance. Close your eyes. How far can you flex before you lose your balance backward? Reaching forward with your arms will help. Practice moving through as long a range as you can until the movement pattern feels comfortable. (If you can't get your hips as low as your knees without losing your balance backward, you might need to modify your boots. See Lower-Leg Angle in chapter 4 and Forward Lean in chapter 10.) Now put on your skis and head for a flat run or road, and make turns in a tuck, as shown in figure 6.12. With every turn you make, move up and down through that long range of movement. Exaggerate! Don't let your vanity keep you from doing something you think looks funny. You learn a movement pattern best by pushing your body to the extremes of the pattern, and this one is no exception. After a run or two in a tuck, make normal turns, still exaggerating the up and down for at least a couple of full runs.

FIGURE 6.12 A good exercise for learning to move straight up and down is to make turns in a tuck, exaggerating the up and down motions. Move up and down as far as you can through each turn. As you flex down into a low tuck, your back should become almost parallel with the snow as you reach forward with your hands. Skier: Toni Sears.

Another excellent exercise is to make traverses through a mogul field, as shown in figure 6.13. In a wide mogul field with little traffic, start by making slow traverses, focusing on flexing and extending so that you feel a consistent amount of pressure under your feet and keeping your center of gravity moving along a straight line. Gradually steepen your traverses, raising your speed. As you get more precise with your movements and feel more comfortable, try jumping an occasional gap between two moguls, landing on the down slope of the far side of the second one.

FIGURE 6.13 Traversing through moguls is excellent for developing vertical flexion and extension. Start slow, and increase your speed as comfort allows. Skier: Brian Blackstock.

Passive and Active Flexing

Under most circumstances, an expert skier absorbs a bump by flexing passively at the knees and waist: relaxing the thigh, buttock, and lower-back muscles, and letting gravity pull the upper body and hips down while the snow pushes the feet and legs up. In some situations, though, the skier must actively contract certain muscles in order to flex quickly enough and still remain balanced fore and aft (figure 6.14). An

FIGURE 6.14 At over 70 mph (110 km/h), Daron Rahlves takes a jump of about 200 feet (60 m) on his way to winning the Birds of Prey Downhill at Beaver Creek, Colorado. Notice that his skis come up off the snow well before he gets to the lip. This indicates he is actively flexing, pulling his legs up and his torso forward and down. In so doing, he reduces the length of his flight and time in the air, which gets him to the finish line sooner. It's crucial on big jumps like this that the skier flex with precision to maintain his balance in the air. All of Daron's flexing is at the knees, hips, and lower back. There is none at the ankles. Rahlves, who won this race, is one of America's most successful World Cup downhillers, and won the 2001 World Championship in super G. He was particularly good in the air, on the hardest snow, and on the steepest pitches.

example is aggressive skiing in deep moguls, in which the force from the snow can increase so quickly that you must actively pull your upper body forward and down to moderate those forces and stay in fore–aft balance (figure 6.15). If you don't, gravity won't pull your upper body forward and down fast enough to compensate for how quickly your legs are being pushed up, and you'll end up on your heels.

FIGURE 6.15 To ski extremely large moguls at high speed, good mogul skiers actively flex their bodies, significantly reducing the force of the bump. The hip flexor muscles, the same ones a diver uses to perform a jackknife, are the ones that do the work. Skier: Jerry Berg.

The hip flexors, primarily the abdominal and iliopsoas muscles, do the work of pulling the trunk forward and the legs up. If the torso isn't facing in exactly the same direction as the feet, as is often the case, the oblique abdominal muscles come into play. Whether the skier is flexing actively or passively, the relative articulations at the major joints are the same. Think of negotiating a corner in a car. Whether you have power steering or not, you have to turn the front wheels the same amount.

Active flexing is part of a movement pattern called *avalement*, from the French word for swallowing. Georges Joubert was the first to identify and analyze this movement in the late 1960s, when he saw Jean-Claude Killy perform it spontaneously in certain situations. Joubert then made avalement a key technique in his training regimens, which produced numerous successful international racers. The movement pattern is more important today than ever.

People watching a world-class mogul skier often remark that the skier's knees and back must take a pounding, because they see a sharp compression of the body as the skier encounters each bump. These skiers don't take nearly the beating you might think because those motions of the body are usually deliberate and proactive. The skier is actively snapping the body into a flexed posture in anticipation of the bump to reduce the force it could exert on him. Viewed from the side, you can see that the skier's feet move up and down, but his center of gravity follows a much straighter line.

Unweighting

The terms commonly used to describe increasing and decreasing the overall force between the snow and the skier are *weighting* and *unweighting*, respectively. The words make sense subjectively, but technically they're misnomers. Your weight might change when you eat a big lunch, but it doesn't change when you fly off a bump into the air. What changes is the magnitude of the force the snow exerts on you. You feel light when you lift off a bump because that force goes away. Conversely, you feel heavier when you ski into a dip because the reaction force from the snow increases. These sensations are produced by vertical accelerations and decelerations of your center of gravity relative to the snow. Technical inaccuracies notwithstanding, we'll use the terms weighting and unweighting here because they make sense to skiers.

Because the initiation phase of many turns is facilitated by unweighting, most systems of ski instruction once emphasized unweighting skills. As the slopes we ski on have become more manicured and our skis easier to turn, focus has shifted to other skills. This is unfortunate for two reasons. First, to ski well in many situations still requires unweighting. Second, it was in learning to unweight that skiers learned to move up and down properly—a skill all good skiers still need. Skiers are, in general, more static on their skis than they were 20 years ago, and the reduced instructional emphasis on unweighting could be a primary reason.

Unweighting comes in two main types: *up-unweighting* and *down-unweighting*. Both can be produced by the skier, variations in terrain, the virtual bump, or combinations of the three. How and when the force changes between the skier and the snow depends on the direction and timing of vertical accelerations of the skier's center of gravity. See figure 6.16.

There are two pairs of definitions for these terms (up-unweighting and down-unweighting) in common use today. One of them says that any unweighting that the skier initiates by extending at the knees and hips is an up-unweighting, and any unweighting in which the skier starts by flexing at the knees and hips is a down-unweighting. The other pair of definitions, and the one I prefer and use in this book, bases the definitions on the direction in which the skier's center of gravity moves.

In this book's terminology, up-unweighting always starts with the skier's center of gravity being pushed and accelerated upward, away from the snow. This happens if the skier pushes the body upward by extending, as shown in figure 6.17 on page 101. It can also happen if a bump, real or virtual, pushes the skier upward, even if the skier reduces that push by flexing at the same time, as shown in figures 6.20 on page 104 and 6.3*a* on page 90. This is common, for example, in mogul skiing, where the skier flexes to absorb a bump that's still big enough to project the body upward. During this time the skier feels heavier. When the upward force decreases or disappears, the skier's upward motion is slowed by gravity, and the force between the skis and the snow is reduced. As the skier's center of gravity subsequently falls back toward the snow, the force remains reduced until the center of gravity's downward motion is slowed and stopped.

Skiers are limited in their ability to reduce the up-unweighting effect of bumps by how much they can shorten the distance between their centers of gravity and their feet. A skier of average height wearing properly configured boots can't reduce that distance by more than about 18 inches (45 cm) by flexing. That is, in moving

FIGURE 6.16 As the skier, who weighs 120 pounds, actively extends upward, the force between her feet and the scale increases (indicated by the increase in her apparent weight), accelerating her upward. Once the upward acceleration ends, the skier is "light" until she slows the downward fall that follows.

from a fully extended stance to a fully flexed one, the feet and center of gravity move no more than about 18 inches (45 cm) closer to each other. This means the skier can't absorb a bump taller than about 18 inches (45 cm) without the center of gravity being pushed upward. The subsequent unweighting is thus still an up-unweighting because it begins with an upward acceleration of the center of gravity.

Down-unweighting begins with the skier's center of gravity accelerating toward the snow (figures 6.18 and 9.20a on p. 153). A skier passing over a drop-off or simply relaxing quickly from a tall stance experiences a down-unweighting. There is no initial upward acceleration of the center of gravity. The force supporting the

FIGURE 6.17 Allison Forsyth of Canada performs a classic up-unweighting, projecting her center of gravity upward by extending at the knee and hip.

FIGURE 6.18 Lindsey Vonn flexes in the transition to completely absorb the virtual bump and momentarily unweight her skis. Figure 9.20a on page 153 is another good example of down-unweighting.

skier's body simply disappears or is dramatically reduced, so the skier's center of gravity accelerates downward. While it accelerates, the force under the skis is reduced.

Up-unweighting and down-unweighting both have their strengths and weaknesses. The main advantage of down-unweighting is that it can happen instantly. No preparatory upward acceleration of the center of gravity, during which the overall pressure against the snow actually increases, is needed.

The advantages up-unweighting has over down-unweighting are its potentially longer duration and the superior control that the skier can exercise over its length and intensity. If you were to drop a tennis ball from your hand, it would be "unweighted" only until it hit the ground. The length of down-unweighting you can impart to the ball is limited by your height. In contrast, if you tossed the ball upward and let it drop, the ball would be light for a longer time. The duration of the up-unweighting is limited only by how high you can throw the ball.

Recall that if a person of average height goes from a very tall stance to a very low one, the center of gravity drops about 18 inches (45 cm). If a skier does this by suddenly relaxing the knee and hip extensor muscles, the resulting down-unweighting lasts only about a third of a second. If, on the other hand, that skier performs an up-unweighting that projects the center of gravity another 2 inches (5 cm) farther above the snow than it would have started in the down-unweighting, the skier will be light almost over twice as long.

Up-unweighting accomplished by extending has other advantages: It allows the muscles that work the hardest in skiing, the quadriceps (thighs) and the gluteals (buttocks), to relax and flush lactate, and it allows the chest to expand so the skier can breath more deeply.

Terrain Unweighting

Terrain unweighting is a term used to describe unweighting produced by bumps or drops rather than the skier's muscles (figure 6.19). Terrain unweighting can be either up-unweighting or down-unweighting.

When the slope suddenly falls away, you experience a down-unweighting, even though you might extend to maintain some pressure on the snow. Conversely, skiers skiing into bumps will experience an up-unweighting if they don't flex quickly and deeply enough to prevent their centers of gravity from being projected upward.

As soon as they get comfortable skiing in small bumps, skiers learn to start turns with the help of the terrain unweighting the bumps provide. From then on, all skiers start a large percentage of their turns on bumps, from tiny lumps just a few inches high to mammoth moguls. Somewhere along the way, they learn when and how to flex to reduce terrain unweighting. It's one of the essential skills that enables them to ski expert terrain.

a

b

FIGURE 6.19 Terrain unweighting. The small mogul in figure *a* provides just enough up-unweighting to make turn initiation easy. The skier augments the effect by extending. In figure *b*, because of his speed and the size of the bump, the skier flexes to reduce the terrain's unweighting effect. Skier: Jerry Berg.

Lindsey Vonn

Although she is usually listed by the media as coming from Vail, Colorado, Lindsey Vonn, the most successful American female racer of all time, began her skiing career in Minnesota, in Erich Sailer's Buck Hill program, which has produced many noteworthy skiers. Lindsey trained with Ski Club Vail in her teens, and her family eventually moved there in the late '90s.

Vonn was a true prodigy, being the only U.S. skier to have won the Trofeo Topolino, a yearly competition in Italy for the best 11- to 14-year-old skiers in the world. She also claimed medals at the Junior World Championships and won U.S. titles while in her teens.

True to her Minnesota roots, she first made the U.S. Ski Team in slalom, but like Cindy Nelson, another world-class skier from Minnesota, Vonn has been most successful at the World Cup level in downhill and super G. After having been successful internationally in the speed events for several years and winning her first overall and downhill titles in 2008, Lindsey focused her attention on the technical events during her summer training. The result? She won the first slalom of the 2008-09 season and followed it with three more slalom podium appearances, including another victory, finishing third in the slalom standings. In all, it was an incredible year, with World Cup titles in the overall (making her the only American woman to win the overall twice), downhill, and super G; second place in combined and third in slalom; and gold medals in the World Championship downhill and super G. She won nine World Cup races, more than any other American has in a single season.

Vonn works her legs independently and sometimes looks knock-kneed, angulating strongly with her outside knee to control its carving while using the inside ski for varying amounts of support. She is also known to be among the best-conditioned athletes on the circuit.

That Lindsey Vonn has accomplished all she has by the age of 24 is remarkable. It also seems quite likely that she will extend the records she now holds and break more of them before she's through.

Rebound

Rebound is a type of up-unweighting that occurs in short radius, checked turns and is commonly used on steeper slopes where speed control is important. As with moguls and sharply carved turns that produce sizable virtual bumps, the unweighting effect of rebound is not produced by a deliberate action on the part of the skier but rather is the result of the dynamics of the turn. And, as with moguls and significant virtual bumps, the skier usually mitigates its unweighting effect by flexing a bit at the knee and hip. Modern shaped skis have reduced the need for rebound, but it remains an important skill for well-rounded skiers.

Rebound employs a sharp, clean edgeset at the end of the turn, resulting in an abrupt increase in the snow's reaction force. The sudden force from the snow and accompanying deceleration of the skier's feet produce two effects that cause the unweighting. The first is an effect something like a pole vault (figure 6.20). The box in which pole vaulters plant their poles is below their centers of gravity. The reaction of the box to the pole and the vaulter redirects the center of gravity into a circular arc with the box at its center. This is the same "pole-vault effect" described in The Virtual Bump in chapter 3 and diagrammed in figure 3.10.

FIGURE 6.20 The pole-vault effect. When a skier goes from being inclined to one side of the feet to the other, the center of gravity is projected upward like that of a pole vaulter. Here, Chemmy Alcott of the British Ski Team flexes to reduce its effect.

The second source of rebound unweighting is a rubber-band effect of the leg and hip extensors: the thigh, buttock, and lower-back muscles. To get the sharp increase in pressure needed for the edgeset, the skier allows the center of gravity to fall toward the feet, then catches it with a quick contraction of those muscles. When the contracting muscles catch the falling mass of the upper body and upper legs, they stretch a bit, then recoil, tossing the center of gravity back upward (figure 6.21).

Contrary to common belief, the skis themselves don't contribute appreciably to rebound through a trampoline effect. Compared to a skier's weight, the skis are simply not stiff enough to store and return much energy. In addition, the skis are supported by the snow directly underneath the skier's feet, unlike a trampoline, which is supported only along its edge.

FIGURE 6.21 A rebound turn. In addition to the pole vault effect, the skier's knee and hip extensors produce a sort of rubber-band rebound. Skier: Bob Barnes.

Choosing the Technique for the Task

With so many techniques available to control the force on you in the transition, it's natural to wonder which ones to use and when. This is where considerations of terrain, snow, and tactics come in. If your line and the dynamics of the turn create a big virtual bump, you'll probably want to flex to absorb it. If you're in inconsistent, unskied snow, you might very well want to up-unweight strongly in the transition between turns to get your skis out of it. The length of the transition between two turns is also a big factor, as described in Estimating the Transition in chapter 9. A long transition favors up-unweighting. If you need to get across your skis and into the next turn as quickly as possible, down-unweighting is your best choice (figure 6.22).

Practice all the techniques until they become second nature. Then, when you go out and ski, focus not on your technique but on your tactics, the snow, and the mountain. Your body will learn to pick the right moves on its own.

FIGURE 6.22 Terrain and tactics dictate the best techniques for managing the total force from the snow. Here we see Didier Cuche of Switzerland winning a giant slalom in front of the home-country crowd at Adelboden. Because he wants to get pressure on his skis early in the turns, he flexes through the transition between the first two turns to absorb a roll, and extends in the next transition because he's skiing into a hollow.

Turning the Skis

Modern shaped skis enable us to carve many more turns than we used to, but as I explained in chapter 3, most turns still require an initial steering angle, dictated by such factors as terrain, turn shape, and pitch. The steeper the slope and the sharper the turn, the greater the initial steering angle that's needed. Expert skiers on ultrasteep and narrow pitches often pivot their skis more than 120 degrees at the start of the turn. The turns in World Cup slalom and giant slalom courses often require racers to begin turns with significant steering angles, too, as Aksel Lund Svindal does in figure 7.1. Because our skis are better today, those initial steering angles are generally smaller than they once were, but they're achieved using the same techniques we used with older, straighter skis: the techniques described in this chapter.

You can redirect your skis in several ways:

- Make the skis oversteer. This is covered in detail in chapters 2 and 5.

- Use internal muscular forces to apply torque to the ski. Most of the techniques in this chapter fall into this category.

- Use a pole plant to get the snow to put a twisting force on your entire body.

All these techniques are useful, and a well-rounded skier uses them all.

FIGURE 7.1 Aksel Lund Svindal of Norway starts this giant slalom turn by turning his skis to a significant initial steering angle, dictated by the set of the course.

Leg Rotation

Leg rotation is the most important technique used today to turn the skis, and the preferred technique for most situations is twisting one or both legs in the hips (figures 7.1, 7.2, and 7.3). When instructors talk about "turning your feet," this is what they mean. This technique is used in skiing maneuvers at all levels, from gliding wedge turns to dynamic parallel turns.

Ski instructors and coaches commonly call this technique *braquage* (pronounced *bra-'kazh*), a French term introduced by Georges Joubert that literally means "steering." If you turn both legs at the same time, or if there's weight on both your feet when you twist one leg inward, your upper body will remain motionless, and you can turn your skis without disturbing your balance.

If, on the other hand, you twist only your outside leg inward and lift your inside foot off the snow, your upper body reacts by turning a bit toward the outside. This sets your upper body into a countered position (described in chapter 4), ready for hip angulation early in the turn. This is a technique racers have used for decades. Rainer Schoenfelder executes such a movement in the fourth and fifth frames of figure 4.14 on page 65. Because his right ski is off the snow, the muscular effort that rotates his left leg inward also causes his upper body to turn slightly toward the outside of the turn.

Leg rotation works well for several reasons. Rotating the leg inward generally rolls the ski on its edge, too, combining the increase of the ski's steering

FIGURE 7.2 **Ted Ligety turns his skis sideways using leg rotation to scrub speed before making a turn.**

FIGURE 7.3 **Leg rotation is used here to steer the skis in short turns. Skier: Carol Levine.**

angle with an increase in the edge and platform angles—often a desirable combination (see figure 8.3, p. 125). Leg rotation is also powerful. With it a skier can produce large torques, and produce them through an entire turn, much longer than any other rotary technique. Leg rotation also allows you to manipulate your skis with your legs alone, leaving your upper body to balance against whatever forces are acting on you. It imparts no angular momentum to your body as a whole, and because it involves the movement of relatively little body mass, leg rotation does little to disturb your balance and stability.

Leg rotation is one of those key techniques of skiing that is, unfortunately, less than obvious to many self-taught skiers. The intuitive movement for most beginners is to twist the upper body and hips in the direction they want their skis to turn—movements that usually have counterproductive side effects. Turning the leg in the hip to the degree that a good skier turns it isn't an essential movement in many sports, which might be why it doesn't come naturally for many beginning skiers.

A straight leg can't exert as much turning force on the ski as a bent one, especially when it's the outside leg. The interior rotators of the femur, which are used when the leg is extended, aren't nearly as strong in this regard as the adductors, which come into play when the leg is bent. As a result, this technique is most powerful when performed from a flexed, athletic stance.

EXERCISE To feel the movement for yourself, sit on the edge of a chair with your feet and knees about 6 inches (15 cm) apart. Now, without moving your heels, twist your right leg so that your right big toe touches your left foot, and your right knee touches your left knee. This movement is the essence of leg rotation. You might feel as if you're twisting your knee, but you're actually turning your femur in your hip.

EXERCISE Two good on-snow exercises are shown in figures 7.4 and 7.5. They will show you the range of motion possible in the hip and help you understand and feel leg rotation. The first is drawing a large C in the snow with your foot (figure 7.4). The other is twisting your legs to scrub bow ties in the snow (figure 7.5). Both exercises use variations of the same motion used in leg rotation: turning the femur in the pelvis. It's worth noting that women typically have a greater range in leg rotation than men.

a

b

c

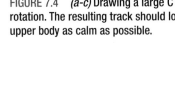

d

FIGURE 7.4 *(a-c)* Drawing a large C in the snow with your foot using leg rotation. The resulting track should look like figure *d*. Keep your hips and upper body as calm as possible.

a   b   c

FIGURE 7.5 *(a-b)* Twisting your legs to scrub bow ties in the snow using leg rotation. The resulting track of one foot is shown in figure *c*. Make the movements by turning just your legs and feet. If you have someone try to hold your feet still while performing the exercise, you'll see how powerful this movement is.

Pivot slips, the exercise described in chapter 5 as a fore–aft balance exercise and demonstrated in figure 5.8 on page 83, is also an excellent exercise for leg rotation. In this case, the focus of the exercise is on keeping the torso and hips facing your direction of travel, and changing the edges of both skis at the same time as they pivot.

EXERCISE

Anticipation

Anticipation, also known as *windup-release*, is a technique used mostly in linked, short radius turns. Although inklings of the movement pattern can be seen in pictures of skiers from the 1950s and earlier, anticipation became commonly visible in the skiing of world-class ski racers in the mid-1960s. To this day, it remains a fundamental element of advanced short-turn technique.

From the fall line to the end of the turn, your legs wind up under your torso, which continues to face more or less down the fall line. The resulting twist in your body through the hips and lower back stretches several muscles, some of them large, including those used for leg rotation. When the skis disengage from the snow, either via unweighting or flattening as they change edges, those stretched muscles seek to shorten, realigning your legs with your upper body (figure 7.6). A blocking pole plant, described in the next section, is usually used to stabilize the upper body so that all the realignment occurs in the legs.

The term *anticipation* refers to the entire windup and release mechanism and can be powered by tension in parts of the body other than those already mentioned. For example, a windup in the knees and lower legs, common in short turns, can be seen in the middle frame of figure 3.7 on page 39. Telemark skiers develop windup tension in the abdominals and lower-back muscles, as shown in figure 7.7.

The muscle tension created by the windup isn't a big source of torque for turning the skis, but it supplies enough to be useful in turns in which the skis are unweighted, or the tips and tails are free of the snow, as is common in moguls, especially when accompanied by a well-planted pole (figures 7.8 and 7.9).

One of anticipation's greatest benefits is that it enhances leg rotation. It places the hips and legs in a relationship that provides the maximum range and power for leg rotation. A muscle will develop its maximum contracting force when it's first stretched to about 120 percent of its resting length, and some of the muscles stretched in the windup phase of anticipation are the same ones used for leg rotation. Thus, the windup enables the skier to perform a more powerful leg rotation. Yet another advantage of anticipation is that it coordinates well with the increased hip angulation and countering that are often effective in the completion phase of short, linked turns. Figure 8.8 on page 129 illustrates this well.

FIGURE 7.6 Anticipation, or windup-release, is an important technique for turning the skis at the start of short radius turns. It is usually used in conjunction with leg rotation and, often, a blocking pole plant. Skier: Charley Stocker.

FIGURE 7.7　Good Telemark skiers use the same basic techniques for turning their skis as those used on alpine equipment. Here we see anticipation, leg rotation, a blocking pole plant, and a bit of upper-body rotation used to steer the skis through the initiation of this turn. Because the Telemark stance constrains the skier's hips to face slightly toward the inside of the turn, the muscular windup created by anticipation occurs completely in the lower torso. There's no windup in the muscles surrounding the heads of the femurs, as there is on alpine equipment. Skier: Patti Banks.

FIGURE 7.8　Anticipation is a technique well suited to moguls, especially when augmented with a blocking pole plant. When the skier's feet reach the crest of the mogul, the tips and tails of the skis aren't restrained by the snow, and the tension in the stretched muscles around the hip joints and lower torso redirects the skis into the turn. Skier: Bob Barnes.

FIGURE 7.9　Because of the anticipation developed at the end of the first turn, this skier's body unwinds in the air, and his skis swing toward the fall line. Notice also how his upper body turns slightly toward the outside. Skier: Josh Fogg.

Torque From the Pole Plant

Planted properly, your pole will do something you might not have thought it could: It will make you turn. You must plant the pole at an angle: When the tip of the pole goes in the snow, it must be ahead of the hand that planted it. This is the critical element that enables the snow to exert a turning force (figures 7.10 and 7.11). All great skiers, from Hannes Schneider to Doug Coombs, have always planted their poles at this angle. With the pole planted obliquely, the snow can push backward on your hand, creating a torque on your entire body about the balance axis. This is called a *blocking pole plant*. If the pole is planted straight up and down, the snow can't do this. Figures 7.12 and 7.13 on page 114 show the physical mechanics involved.

The ability of the snow to apply a torque to the skier is important in short radius turns. It becomes critical on very steep slopes where significant rotary force must be applied to the skis to achieve big initial steering angles.

You can precisely and instantaneously control the amount of torque the pole plant produces by controlling the strength and duration of the contraction of your arm and shoulder muscles. The more firmly they contract, the greater the torque you'll get. The longer the muscles are contracted, the longer that torque is exerted on you. The farther away from the balance axis you plant the pole, the greater the torque will be. You should plant the pole at least a foot and a half (half a meter) away from your body.

FIGURE 7.10 The pole plant is an essential technique for applying rotary forces to the skis. To be effective, the pole must be planted at an angle, with the tip ahead of the hand. Skier: David N. Oliver.

FIGURE 7.11 All the important elements of a good pole plant can be seen in the ones made by these World Cup competitors: *(a)* Ivica Kostelic, *(b)* Maria Riesch, *(c)* Lindsey Vonn, *(d)* Benjamin Raich, *(e)* Manfred Pranger, *(f)* Nicole Hosp, *(g)* Therese Borssen, and *(h)* Kalle Palander.

FIGURE 7.12 When the skier plants her pole, the snow exerts a reaction force on her. Because that force acts along a line that doesn't go through her center of gravity, it creates a torque on her. Skier: Eileen Brown.

FIGURE 7.13 The force that the snow exerts on the skier through his pole, S, has a component that pushes straight up on the skier, S_u, and another that pushes backward, S_b. Because S_b pushes on the skier along a line that doesn't go through his center of gravity, it creates a torque on him. And because S_b is perpendicular to the skier's balance axis, that's the axis about which that torque will make him turn. The size of S_b is determined by the angle at which the pole is planted. If the pole is vertical, S_b is zero, and there is no torque on the skier. That's why the pole must be planted at an angle if it's to make the skier turn. Skier: Andy Gould.

In addition to planting your pole at the correct angle and in the correct place, you must plant it solidly in the snow, and at the right moment (figure 7.14). That moment is at the edge change, when your skis are flat on the snow and you have the best opportunity to pivot them. This means you have to begin the movement of planting your pole earlier, so it will be in the snow, up to the basket, when the edge change occurs.

Here are some common errors skiers make with their pole plants:

1. Planting the pole too late. Instead of planting it at the moment when torque is needed to redirect the skis, the skier plants the pole after starting into the turn (figure 7.15).

2. Planting the pole vertically instead of obliquely. The snow can't produce a torque on the skier about the balance axis unless it's planted obliquely (figure 7.15).

3. Not getting the outside hand in position to plant the pole early enough in the turn. This error usually results in a late pole plant, and the quick arm movement needed to get the pole ready to plant often disturbs the skier's balance.

4. Planting the pole too close to the body. This gives the force from the snow a short lever arm on the skier, reducing the torque from the pole plant. The pole should be at least a foot and a half (half a meter) away from the body.

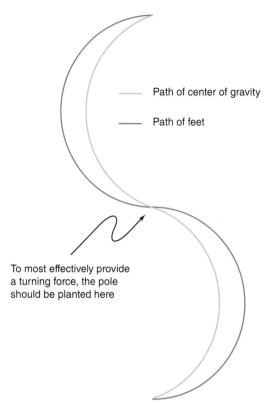

Path of center of gravity

Path of feet

To most effectively provide a turning force, the pole should be planted here

FIGURE 7.14 To be most effective at providing a turning force, the pole plant should be made when the skis are flat on the snow. This occurs at the very start of a turn, or at the inflection point between linked turns when the skier's body moves across the skis.

A good pole plant also enhances the effects of leg rotation and anticipation. Imagine grabbing the ends of a 12-inch (30 cm) piece of garden hose and giving one end a good twist. If you now let go of both ends, they'll both turn as the hose unwinds. If, on the other hand, you let go of only one end, it will turn twice as far as it did when you let go of both ends. Anticipation, discussed earlier, winds your body up like that piece of garden hose. When the skis change edges or are unweighted, they are released from the snow, like the end of the released garden hose. Just as the tension in the hose caused both ends to rotate when they were both released, your upper

FIGURE 7.15 This skier plants his pole after he has started his turn. This error, combined with the fact that the pole is planted straight up and down, makes his pole plant ineffective in providing any turning force. In this case, the skier makes up for this with a stem.

body will turn toward the outside of the turn when the leg turns inward, as shown in figure 7.9 (p. 111)—unless, that is, your upper body is stabilized by a blocking pole plant. In that case, your upper body can't turn toward the outside, so all the twisting force is applied to the ski.

If you lack an effective pole plant, you'll often compensate with some form of hip or upper-body rotation (described in the next section), with a rotary pushoff from the downhill ski to the new outside ski, or by stemming the uphill ski. Adding a good pole plant to your tool kit can make your short turns more crisp and controlled.

Leg rotation, anticipation, and an oblique blocking pole plant are complementary techniques. Together they synergistically constitute the most effective package for creating the initial steering angle for high-end, short radius turns (see figure 7.6, p. 110).

Upper-Body Rotation

Upper-body rotation is a classic technique for pivoting the skis and creating a steering angle. It is intuitive and powerful. Many books on skiing from the 1940s, 1950s, and earlier have beautiful black and white photographs of expert skiers rotating their way through billows of untracked powder. This was the technique taught in Hannes Schneider's Arlberg Ski School, founded in 1921 and generally considered the first ski school with a systematic method of instruction.

These skiers swung the whole upper body—arms, shoulders, and all—into the turn. It worked well at powering their long, stiff wooden skis through the ungroomed and often unpacked snow. All well-rounded skiers still use this technique at one time or another. Often, an expert powder skier will throw off a full-on shoulder rotation to deal with a situation that calls for a lot of torque, as shown in figure 7.16. But

FIGURE 7.16 To start a turn that requires a lot of torque, as in this case where the skier doesn't have much speed and needs to make a fairly short turn in loose snow, upper-body rotation is a good tool to use, along with a blocking pole plant. Notice that she does not commit the common error of throwing her shoulders toward the center of the turn. Skier: Cait Boyd.

when skiing on modern skis that turn easily on snow groomed the night before by cutting-edge machinery, big rotations are overkill. Small rotations, however, are still used by the best skiers to provide small torques when needed. But these skiers are very precise and controlled in their use of the technique. In particular, the movement is restricted to a rotation in the transverse plane about the balance axis. The best skiers never tip their shoulders into the turn, which is a common and serious error on hard snow. In recent years, some of the world's best slalom skiers have started making upper-body rotation movements in the transition, but their purpose is to set the torso up early for the next turn's control phase rather than to power a redirection of the skis. See figure 7.17.

Upper-body rotation involves projecting the outside arm, shoulder, or both in the direction of the intended turn (figure 7.18). The movement starts with a preparation phase in which the arm and shoulder are drawn back. This is followed by a projection phase in which the arm, possibly followed by the shoulder and even the hip, is thrown forward and around in the direction of the new turn. Once the thrown upper-body segments have gained some momentum, they are caught by the contraction of appropriate muscles in the blocking phase, locking them to the rest of the body. This transfers the momentum of the projected body segments to the rest of the body and the skis as a torque.

FIGURE 7.17 Ted Ligety turns his upper body down the hill here not to redirect his skis but to "stay ahead of the course" by setting himself up as early as possible for the control phase of the next turn. He turns his torso and moves it forward to the position it will be in when he strikes the pole, but no further.

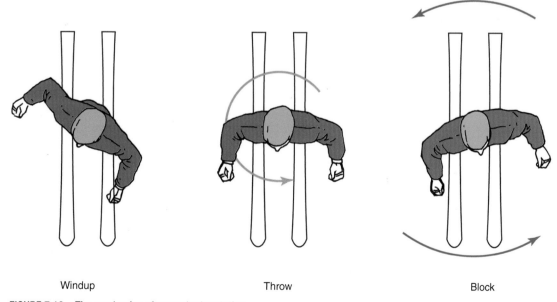

Windup   Throw   Block

FIGURE 7.18 **The mechanics of upper-body rotation.**

The skis must be engaged with the snow during the windup and throw. Otherwise, the rest of the body will counterrotate in a direction opposite that of the projected body segment. For the rotation to have the greatest pivoting effect on the skis, they should be disengaged from the snow at the time the thrown body segment is blocked.

To get a feel for the power and elegance of upper-body rotation, troll the used bookstores in your town for ski books from the mid-1950s or earlier. You'll see a technique well matched to the equipment, snow, and sensibilities of the era, when skiing was a vigorous, adventurous, and romantic sport pursued by true outdoor enthusiasts.

Hip Rotation

In hip rotation (or hip projection, as it's sometimes called), the skier initiates the turn by pushing the hips to the outside of the new turn. This flattens the skis, making it easier to slip the tails out to a good-sized steering angle, even if the skis are pressed against the snow. The movement of the hips can also produce a twisting force on the skis, like upper-body rotation. This is an effective and perfectly acceptable technique in loose snow, particularly at slower speeds or on flatter terrain, where flattening the skis helps them move laterally through the snow. An example can be seen in figure 13.4 on page 196.

To begin using hip rotation effectively in powder, imagine your body as a big corkscrew: The point of the corkscrew is between your feet, and your entire torso, from the hips up, is the handle. Remaining flexed at the knees and waist if possible, twist the handle of the corkscrew with your hips in the direction you want to turn. Avoid tipping your body or shoulders into the turn. Just make big torques by cranking the corkscrew straight down into the snow. Remember that this is a specialized technique used in special situations. When you leave the powder and crud behind, leave the big hip rotation there, too.

Hip rotation is useful in small doses to start turns on packed snow, too. You can use it to deliberately make your skis slip or to help get them to your desired initial steering angle if you don't have enough leg rotation, anticipation, or torque from a blocking pole plant. But you must bring your hips back to the inside of the turn to counter and angulate properly before you reach the fall line or need the skis to grip. Skiers whose boots are overcanted (discussed in chapter 10) sometimes use this technique to get their turns going. Unfortunately, most skiers who start their turns with hip rotation never make the proper midturn adjustment and are left facing their tips with no hip angulation or counter, and underedged skis. This leads to an overreliance on knee angulation and difficulty making short, quick turns because the upper body is turning with the skis. (Hip and knee angulation are discussed in chapter 8, p. 124.)

Short turns are difficult using hip or upper-body rotation because the rotation gives your whole body angular momentum. This takes some time to get going, and also some time to stop, which works against the rhythm of short turns. Also, both types of rotation make your upper body follow your skis through the turn, making short turns that much harder. Great skiers can start a turn with an emergency rotation, then quickly bring everything back together for the rest of the turn, but most skiers suffer through the whole turn with the ill effects of the initiation.

Counterrotation

Counterrotation is a mechanism for turning the skis when they're free of the snow, or nearly flat on it. By rotating the upper body in one direction, the legs and skis naturally turn in the other direction—a technique that animals use intuitively when they're airborne. The technique comes naturally for skiers, too, often showing up in moguls, terrain parks, and other situations in which the skis are off the snow (figures 7.19 and 7.20).

FIGURE 7.19   This skier uses counterrotation to turn his skis as he grinds this rail. He prepares by winding up his upper body in the direction he wants his skis to turn; then, once his skis are in the air and there's no resistance to their turning, he quickly twists his upper body in the opposite direction, causing his skis to turn. In terms of physical mechanics, this technique works because of the principle of conservation of angular momentum.

FIGURE 7.20   After being projected off the snow by a small bump at the end of the first turn, Anja Paerson of Sweden counterrotates with her upper body to turn her skis.

Anja Paerson

Through most of this decade, fans of ski racing were treated to a great rivalry between two great skiers: Anja Paerson of Sweden and Janica Kostelic of Croatia. In the six years from 2001 to 2006, Kostelic's last season, between them they won the overall World Cup five times, the slalom title five times, the giant slalom cup three times, and the combined crown four times. But while the two of them are great technicians, they have distinctly different styles. Where Janica was a technical perfectionist who rarely pushed her line to the point that she needed to make recoveries or adjustments, Anja was, and still is, a fiercely aggressive skier who pushes her line to the limit and who knows how to stay fast while recovering from a bobble. This is not to say that she's a reckless thrasher who improvises her way through the course. On the contrary, she is technically outstanding, and that is one of the keys to her ability to cope with the unexpected. When she takes a risky line, she goes into it with her hands up, level, and out in front, so if she gets thrown unexpectedly, it's from a solid, balanced place. Her strength, agility, technique, and tactics have won her 40 World Cup races.

Anja comes from Tarnaby, a small town in the north of Sweden within one degree of latitude of the Arctic Circle, also the hometown of Ingemar Stenmark. As Paerson tells it, skiing was what there was to do, so that's what she did. She won her first World Cup race at the age of 17. And considering that Tarnaby's skiing facilities are small, served by just two T-bars, it's no surprise that the win was a slalom. She soon found success in giant slalom, too. In 2005, like many of the great skiers, she began to find herself on the downhill and super G podiums. Truly one of the great all-around skiers, she is the only person, man or woman, to have won a World Championship title in all five disciplines, which was sealed with her victory in the 2007 World Championship downhill at Aare, Sweden. Her capture of five total medals—three gold—in her home country was particularly sweet.

Putting It Together on the Hill

Certain techniques for turning the skis are better than others, depending on the situation. But rarely are they used in isolation. An expert skier has a mastery of all the techniques presented in this chapter, and mixes and matches them as the need arises, often in the same turn, as shown in figure 7.21.

FIGURE 7.21　In these turns we see several mechanisms used to turn the skis. Leg rotation, anticipation, blocking pole plants, and a bit of upper-body rotation complement each other to produce great skiing. Skier: Cait Boyd.

Edging the Skis

All skiers learn early on the importance of edging skills. Ask them what they do to make their skis turn, and many shrug their shoulders. Ask them how they edge their skis, and they crank their knees in. Ski flex, sidecut, and torsion are subtleties underappreciated by most skiers, but everyone understands sharp edges.

In this chapter we'll discuss how to control those edges. When you think about edge control, you probably think about how to make edges hold on hard snow, or how to keep from catching edges in moguls or rough snow conditions. Just as important, you need to be able to release your edges so that your skis slip in a controlled and predictable way, change edges smoothly as you go from turn to turn, and adjust your skis' edge angle to control the radius of your turns.

How to Make a Ski Hold

Intuition tells you that big edge angles make your skis hold. The bigger, the better. It's easy to draw this conclusion. After all, the harder you crank your knees into the turn, the better your skis seem to grip. In this case your intuition is wrong. Recall from chapter 2 that for the ski to hold, it just needs to cut a small platform in the snow, and that platform has to be at an angle of 90 degrees or less to a line from it to your center of gravity (see The Ski's Platform Angle in chapter 2). This, along with the edge being sufficiently sharp, is the first key to making the ski hold.

The second key is properly aligning your ankle in the frontal plane so you can hold the ski at that angle while you make all the other fundamental movements of skiing. Have you ever wondered how an ice skate holds? Skates are not nearly as stiff and powerful as ski boots, and the ice in any rink is as hard as the worst boiler plate a skier is ever likely to see. Yet a casual skater can cut clean arcs on a rink, but good skiers often struggle to hold turns on snow that's not nearly as hard. The difference lies in the relative locations of the ankle and the weight-bearing edge, viewed in the frontal plane. Those relative locations, the alignment of the forces on the edge and the ankle, and how they vary is at the heart of edging technique in skiing. Figure 8.1 has a number of parts, each of which explains how these issues of force and alignment bear on one of the topics in this chapter. We'll refer back to this figure as each of those topics comes up.

The blade of an ice skate is directly under the center of the skater's ankle (figure 8.1*a*). So when the skate is on edge, the force that the ice exerts on the blade passes directly through the center of the skater's ankle.

The force from the snow on the edge of a ski, in contrast, is offset from the center of the skier's ankle and creates a torque on it that tries to flatten the ski, as shown in figure 8.1*b*. The force from the snow, *S*, acts along a line that passes outside the skier's ankle. The distance from that line to the skier's ankle, *r*, creates a lever arm through which *S* exerts a torque (see the yellow arrow in figure 8.1) on the ankle. This torque seeks to twist the skier's ankle, flattening the ski on the snow. The

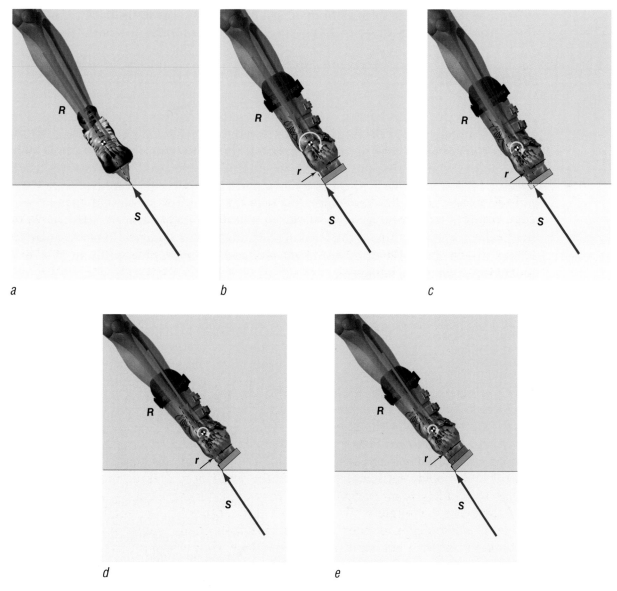

FIGURE 8.1 How well you can make an ice skate or skis hold on ice and snow is directly related to where your ankle is in relation to force exerted by the ice or snow on the edge you're standing on. *(a)* An ice skate holds well because the edge is directly under the center of the skater's ankle, in the frontal plane. *(b)* A ski's edge is offset from the center of the skier's ankle. This puts a torque on the skier's ankle that works to make the ski flatten and slip. *(c)* On softer snow, the ski penetrates farther, bringing the force from the snow, *S*, closer to the center of the ankle, reducing the torque that tries to flatten the ski. *(d)* By angulating, the skier brings the ankle closer to the line along which the force from the snow acts. This reduces the torque on the ankle, enabling the skier to hold it on edge. *(e)* By raising the ankle farther above the edge, a binding lift or plate amplifies the effect of angulation, reducing the torque further. The skier in this figure is angulated to the exact same degree as the skier in figure *d*, but the torque on the ankle is smaller.

longer *r* is, the greater this torque will be. Unless this torque is completely resisted by the ski boot and the muscles supporting the ankle, the ski's platform angle will increase, and if that angle exceeds 90 degrees, the ski will slip.

The second key to holding, then, is to make the ski work more like a skate: to get the center of the ankle as close as possible to the line along which the force from the snow acts so that the torque on the ankle is as small as possible, and therefore easier to resist. This is why skis that are narrow under the foot hold better than wide ones. It's also why skis hold well in soft snow: As the ski is driven farther into the snow surface, as shown in figure 8.1*c*, the force from the snow moves closer to the center line of the ski, making the lever arm on the ankle shorter and reducing the torque on it. You use movements of angulation, described next, to control the distance between the center of the ankle and the line of force of the snow pushing against the ski.

Angulation

Angulation is the general name for several movement patterns that create angles in the skier's body at certain joints when viewed in the frontal plane. These angles have the effect of controlling the alignment of the ankle with the force on the ski's edge, and to what degree the ski behaves more like an ice skate (figure 8.1*d*). Each specific type of angulation also has its own particular purpose, too, which we'll get to later. As skis and boots have improved over the years, the amount of angulation a skier needs in most turns has lessened, but it's still there. And until either the laws of physics or the structure of the human body changes, it always will be. Angulation comes in two major flavors, *knee angulation* and *hip angulation*, with an available seasoning of *ankle angulation*.

FIGURE 8.2　Knee angulation. By rotating the femur inward, the ankle moves closer to the line of action of the force from the snow. Skier: David N. Oliver.

Knee Angulation

In addition to helping align the ankle with the force on the ski, knee angulation performs the important function of adjusting the ski's edge and platform angles. Technically speaking, knee angulation moves the knee laterally without moving the center of gravity or the inclination of the balance axis. In everyday terms, knee angulation means cranking your knee in, a movement that comes naturally to skiers. It's a movement they make intuitively when they want the ski to hold better.

We call it knee angulation because it produces an angle in your body at the knee when viewed in the frontal plane (figure 8.2). Physiologically, your femur is turning in the ball-and-socket joint it makes with your pelvis. The knee, a hinge joint, can't flex inward to any appreciable degree. The hip joint's freedom of motion and the powerful muscles that control it enable the skier to turn the leg inward while bent to angulate at the knee.

EXERCISE

Sit on the edge of your chair with your feet about 12 inches (30 cm) apart. Without moving or turning your feet, bring one knee over to touch the other. This is knee angulation. You'll notice that your foot went up on its edge, and that your ankle is now over that edge. You might also notice that this movement is similar to, but slightly different from, leg rotation, explained in chapter 7 (see figure 8.3).

FIGURE 8.3   Jean-Baptiste Grange uses the similar movements of knee angulation and leg rotation in combination.

The muscles used for knee angulation vary with the posture of the leg, just as they do when performing leg rotation. When the leg is fairly extended, the medial rotators of the femur in the pelvis roll the outside ski up onto its inside edge. When the leg is flexed, the femur's adductors, which are much stronger, do the work. This suggests that you'll be able to hold the ski on edge more effectively under a load when you're in an aggressive, low stance.

Too much knee angulation can be a bad thing. Remember that the knee is a hinge joint, and if it's brought too far inside of the force on the ski, that force can make the knee bend in ways it wasn't meant to. Trying to absorb a large mogul with the knee cranked far to the inside, for example, can be dangerous. Just how much knee angulation is best for you is a matter of skeletal and muscular alignment. With the ski at a platform angle of 90 degrees, the middle of your knee should be aligned with, or a bit inside of, a line from your center of gravity to your edge when viewed in the frontal plane, and your ankle should be close to that line. Achieving this alignment is mostly a matter of boot setup (covered in chapter 10).

EXERCISE

An exercise to help you feel the how and why of knee angulation is shown in figure 8.4. Stand on a hard, level step in your ski boots, as shown in the figure. Move one of your feet so it overhangs the step, and you're standing on just the very edge of the boot sole. With the majority of your weight on that foot, slowly move your knee left and right. You'll feel the torque on your knee and ankle change as they get closer to and farther from the line between your center of gravity and the edge of the step. That's knee angulation at work.

a   b

FIGURE 8.4   With this exercise you'll feel how knee angulation reduces the torque on your ankle and makes it easier to hold an edge.

FIGURE 8.5   Hip angulation. The hips move toward the inside of the turn while the upper torso moves toward the outside, aligning the force on the outside ski with the head of the femur in the frontal plane while moving the ankle closer to that force. Skier: Eileen Brown.

Hip Angulation

As we saw in chapter 4, hip angulation has an important purpose beyond helping get the ankle close to the force on the edge. It also moves the head of the outside femur into the line between your center of gravity and the edge of your outside ski, when viewed in the frontal plane (figure 8.5). Hip angulation moves the head of the femur laterally toward the inside of the turn in coordination with a movement of the shoulders to the outside so that the center of gravity doesn't move laterally at all. Unlike knee angulation, hip angulation doesn't come naturally, and self-taught skiers often lack hip-angulation skills. To accelerate your progress, pay close attention to how you angulate at the hips. This isn't to say that hip angulation is more important than knee angulation—just that knee angulation comes more naturally. Also, as described in chapter 4 (p. 73), counter is coordinated with hip angulation to bring the best muscles into play for the job of supporting the body.

To get an idea of what hip angulation and counter feel like, perform these exercises, shown in figure 8.6. Stand in your ski boots with your right foot on the very edge of a hard step like you did in the knee-angulation exercise. Reach down with your right hand and touch the side of your right knee (figure 8.6a). You should feel two things: first, that there's a bit less torque on your ankle, and second, that most of your weight is now on your right foot. That's basic hip angulation.

Now, let your right hand hang free and slide your left foot forward a few inches (5-10 cm), then reach down with your left hand and touch your right kneecap (figure 8.6b). You should feel as much, if not more, weight on your right foot, and you should feel that, rather than bending sideways at the waist, you're folding forward. What you've done is countered. By moving your left foot forward and reaching across with your left hand, you turned your pelvis on top of your femur in the transverse plane and flexed forward at the waist. If you now move your right knee inward until you feel that there's no serious torque on your right ankle, you'll feel a reasonable approximation of the knee angulation, hip angulation, and counter that you might use at the end of a hard turn.

a *b*

FIGURE 8.6 This exercise will show you how hip angulation and countering work.

Ankle Angulation

Some skiers talk about angulating with their ankles to control the ski's edge. Provided the boot allows the movement, everting the foot—rolling it so the sole turns outward—will move the center of the ankle closer to the force on the ski, helping the ski to hold. Everting the foot also makes the boot fit tighter because you're wedging the foot and ankle into the boot at an off-angle. Some world-class racers, including Bode Miller, have been known to deliberately punch bulges in the shells of their boots over the navicular bone (or scaphoid) to provide increased mobility in this mode. That said, many of the best athletes prefer boots that allow little or no movement of the foot and ankle.

Coordinating Knee and Hip Angulation

Both knee and hip angulation are needed to bring the ankle as close as possible to the force on the ski in a well-carved turn. Hip angulation also serves to help properly align the outside hip joint with that line, and knee angulation provides fine-tuning of the edge and platform angles. Great skiers vary in the proportion of knee and hip angulation they use, but everyone uses some of each (figure 8.7). It's also not unusual to see a particular athlete's style of angulation evolve over time, especially if the athlete changes boot suppliers.

a

b

FIGURE 8.7   Jean-Baptiste Grange and Ted Ligety are two of the best male slalom skiers in the world. They also have distinctly different styles when it comes to angulation. *(a)* Grange uses less hip angulation and counter, resulting in a stance that's fairly square to his skis, and relies heavily on knee angulation. *(b)* In the same gate, Ligety clearly is more countered and angulated at the hip. The skiers were 0.1 second apart in this section of the course, and just over 0.2 second apart for the run.

The amount of hip or knee angulation appropriate for an individual has a lot to do with personal morphology—the relative mass distribution between the upper torso and midbody, the distance between the hip sockets, and the angle between the femur and tibia in the frontal plane (the Q angle), for example. Because there is more variation among women in this regard than men, there is more variation in their angulation styles, too.

In short radius turns, which usually depend on leg rotation early in the turn, you should feel that the leg rotation blends directly into knee angulation. Hip angulation comes later in the turn, as you come out of the fall line, as much the result of your legs winding up under your body as an active movement with your upper body (figure 8.8).

In medium and large radius turns (figure 8.9, p. 130), which don't often require much leg rotation, you should turn the upper body toward the outside early in the turn to establish a countered position in the turn's initiation phase. As the ski begins to load up entering the control phase, move the hips toward the inside of the turn as you move your shoulders to the outside, then turn the outside knee (and in some cases the inside knee, too) inward to tighten up the platform angle and ankle alignment until the edge is felt to be slicing the snow cleanly. Finally, in the completion phase, your hip angulation and counter will decrease (see chapter 4) as the outside foot moves forward and you begin the transition to the next turn, which requires countering in the other direction.

FIGURE 8.8 Anja Paerson's hip angulation develops progressively as she carves through a slalom turn. Note that the hip angulation and counter also provide anticipation (explained in chapter 7) to help turn the skis in the initiation of the second turn.

FIGURE 8.9 Entering a giant slalom turn, Fredrik Nyberg of Sweden counters, turning his hips and torso toward the outside of the turn. This aligns him to angulate and balance over the outside ski in the upcoming control phase of the turn.

Releasing the Edge by De-Angulating

As the ability of skis to hold has improved since the late 1990s, the ability to make them slip in a controlled, predictable way has become an important skiing skill. More and more, skiers talk about "feathering the edge" to make the ski slip when they want to adjust their line in the middle of a turn or scrub a little speed. Depending on where the skier is balanced fore and aft, the whole ski might slip sideways, or it might oversteer. When the ski is flattened, the skier can also steer it with a bit of hip or leg rotation.

On traditional skis, this was easy: The skier just reduced angulation, and the ski slipped. Using modern shaped carving skis and aggressive boots, the skier must often do more: De-angulate to increase the skis' platform angle. This is often useful in moguls, slalom and giant slalom racing, and on steep slopes (figures 8.10 and 7.17 on p. 117).

Most commonly, this de-angulation is done by pushing the hips to the outside of the turn, in a movement that could also include a slight hip rotation. The legs can also be rotated toward the outside of the turn, de-angulating at the knees.

a   b

FIGURE 8.10 Making the skis slip when you want them to is an important skill. *(a)* Benjamin Raich pushes his hip out in the third and fourth frames to make his skis slip and scrub speed, then in the fifth frame brings the hip back in to make the ski hold. *(b)* This skier makes a similar move with his hip in slushy snow; in this case his purpose is to slide up to a good spot to make a braking edgeset. Skier: Dan Egan.

Effects of Ski Design and Binding Lifters on Edging

Sondre Norheim made and competed on skis with sidecut in Telemark, Norway, in the 1860s. (It is often said that these were the first skis to have sidecut, but that's not the case.) They were 70 millimeters wide at the waist. By 1970, skis had narrowed a bit. The Rossignol Strato, a premier slalom racing ski of the time, was 68 millimeters wide. For the 2008-09 season, slalom race skis used in World Cup competition can be as narrow as 63 millimeters wide at the waist. By becoming narrower, racing skis have become more like ice skates, as explained earlier in this chapter. (The Fédération Internationale de Ski [FIS], the governing body of international ski competition, today sets limits on the minimum width of racing skis as well as the length of slalom skis and minimum sidecut radius of giant slalom, super G, and downhill skis, citing safety concerns.) The FIS limits are constantly pushed by manufacturers and competitors, and racers have been disqualified for competing on skis only a millimeter below the minimum. In fact, one of the factors that limits the useful lifetime of World Cup race skis is how many times they can be filed without making them illegally narrow (figure 8.11).

Mounting the bindings on lifts or dampening plates (figure 8.12)—which are also used to improve the vibration characteristics of race skis—improves edging by lifting the ankle farther from the edge of the ski. Figure 8.1*e* shows the effect of increasing the height of the boot sole above the snow with a plate or lift under the binding. The center of the ankle has been brought closer to the line of action of the force on the ski, further reducing the torque on the ankle. This is what skiers who use such lifts and plates commonly describe as increased leverage on the edge.

a   *b*

FIGURE 8.11 The dimensions of skis used in World Cup competition are regularly measured by FIS officials to ensure they conform to the rules. Here, the sidecut radius of a downhill ski is being checked to make certain that it's not smaller than the legal limit.

In addition to regulating ski widths, FIS has imposed a limit on how far the boot sole can be above the snow, again due to safety concerns. In response, boot manufacturers provided their athletes with more lift by making the soles of their boots thicker, to which FIS quickly responded by limiting the height the competitor's heel can be above the sole of the boot.

Precise measurements are taken seriously by both competitors and the rule-setters (figure 8.13). Ted Ligety was disqualified from the super combined event of the 2009 FIS World Championships, an event in which he was a serious contender for a medal, because the height of his boot sole from the bottom of the ski measured 0.15 millimeters over the limit. As Ligety explained, "Every person on the tour takes that rule to the absolute limit, because every millimeter counts as far as creating angles and leverage on your skis."

FIGURE 8.12 The plate beneath the binding lifts the skier's ankle farther from the ski's edge. This amplifies the effects of angulation.

FIGURE 8.13 This device is being used to measure the thickness of the heel of a World Cup competitor's boot. The maximum height of the heel above the boot's sole is strictly regulated.

The Look of Modern Edging

Advancements in skis, boots, and binding systems over the decades have enabled racers to carve sharper turns, which demand that the skier balance against greater centrifugal forces. The result is an overall look of progressively more inclination and less knee angulation (figure 8.14). Interestingly, hip angulation doesn't seem to have changed as much one way or the other. Keep in mind, however, that the same skills and movements are required to ski well today as they were 30 years ago. The need for amplitude in those movements has been replaced with a need for subtlety and finesse.

a

b

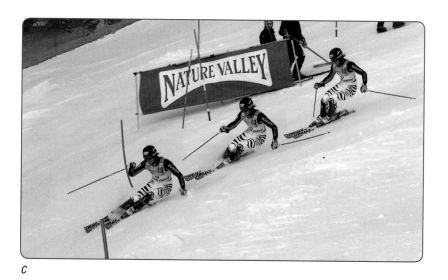

c

FIGURE 8.14 *(a)* Gustavo Thoeni of Italy in 1976. Considered by many to be the most technically important skier of his time, Thoeni was the one against whom all others were measured from the early 1970s until Ingemar Stenmark's arrival on the World Cup circuit. *(b)* Sarah Schleper of the United States, racing in December 1997, using the last generation of traditionally shaped slalom skis. Sarah has much less knee angulation than Thoeni, somewhat less hip angulation, more inclination, and higher edge angle. *(c)* Felix Neureuther of Germany in December 2006. We see the trend continue with less knee angulation, a bit less hip angulation, and significantly more inclination and edge angle. Neureuther, the son of German skiing greats Christian Neureuther and Rosi Mittermaier, is part of the current new wave of slalom skiers who grew up on shaped skis and is making inroads to the top ranks of the World Cup.

Ted Ligety

American Ted Ligety broke onto the World Cup with the leading edge of the first wave of skiers who spent their teenage years on shaped skis. Born in 1984, he and his contemporaries—among them Jean-Baptiste Grange, Felix Neureuther, and Jens Byggmark—have brought a level of innovation and excitement to the technical events that has energized racers and fans alike.

A product of the Park City Ski Education Foundation in Utah, he started scoring points in his first season on the World Cup and was immediately noticed by race watchers for the radical degrees of inclination and edge angle he was holding on the hardest snow. Attention on Ted increased in his second full season on the World Cup, with four trips to the podium and numerous top-10 finishes in slalom. The big story was Ted's Olympic gold medal in the combined event at the 2006 games in Torino, which put him in the spotlight for a broader public. In the 2006-07 season, he started to find his legs in giant slalom, and the next year he won the World Cup title in that discipline.

In his first couple of years on the World Cup, it seemed that Ted's focus on high edge angles and ultratight arcs was not always optimal. Since then, his skiing has evolved, and he comes forward more in the transition so he can now begin carving very early in the turn with minimal initial steering angles. He still holds tighter arcs with more inclination than almost anyone else, and is often seen supporting himself briefly on his pole guards in some slalom turns.

Ligety is one of those athletes who just seems to love racing. His attitude is consistently upbeat, and he is good friends with many of his closest competitors. That easy-going demeanor is probably one reason why Ted does well in second runs. Time and again he has come from behind after the first run to crush the field in the second. Being behind just gives him more incentive to shred.

CHAPTER 9

Lateral Balance

If I were to pick one aspect of ski technique that, more than any other, differentiates skiers of different abilities, it would be how they balance against the lateral force from the snow, and in particular the component that makes them turn. Novices ski with their feet apart because their lateral balance is uncertain. At the other end of the spectrum are experts who can vary the width of their stance at will, and balance entirely on one ski at a time when necessary. Many skiers who fall between these two skill levels want nothing more than to ski with their feet glued together, because they sense that doing so requires skills they don't have, which is true: The ability to ski in a narrow stance depends on good lateral balance skills. One of skiing's ironies is that focusing on keeping your feet together isn't likely to help you develop those skills. Rather, developing an effective, functional technique in which your feet are separated by at least a hand's width and your legs work independently is one of the most reliable ways to develop your lateral balance skills and thereby increase your overall level of skiing.

Balancing Against Centrifugal Force

Back in chapter 1 we saw that an object will be stable as long as the sum of all forces acting on its center of gravity cancel each other out. The snowboarder and skier in the examples we used had only two forces acting on them: gravity pulling down on them, and the force of a terrain park rail pushing up. The issue was whether or not those forces were lined up with each other, and the gravitational force on them passed through their base of support, the rail.

Take a look back at figure 1.12*a* on page 13. During a turn, another important force comes into play: the lateral force from the snow that makes you turn. This is what you experience as centrifugal force. Both centrifugal force and gravity act on you, and their combined resultant force on your center of gravity acts at an angle, along a line inclined into the turn. That line is the balance axis. Gravity's effect is constant, but as figure 3.9 on page 41 shows, centrifugal force changes all the time, which means the resultant force acting on you changes, too. The tighter the turn, the greater the centrifugal force, and the more inclined the resultant force. For you to remain stable, that resultant force *(R)* must still pass through your base of support: the area enclosed by your skis. This means your center of gravity and your balance axis must be inclined into the turn, too.

If your stance is wide, you have a lot of leeway. It's easy to keep the resultant within your base of support. Skiing in a narrower stance, your base of support is smaller. As a result, you have to estimate more accurately how much centrifugal force you'll encounter and more accurately incline your body into the turn so that your center of gravity and feet are precisely aligned with the resultant.

How much centrifugal force a turn generates is determined by many complex factors, including the condition of the snow, the design of the ski, and the ski's steering and edge angles, just to name a few. That skiers can figure this out on the fly is amazing in itself. Inexperienced skiers don't know how much centrifugal force they'll encounter from moment to moment in a turn, so they don't know exactly where the resultant force on their centers of gravity will point. To provide a margin of safety, developing skiers maintain a wide base of support, first with a wedge and then with a wide-track parallel stance. They keep a significant amount of weight on the inside foot going into every turn and simply wait for lateral force to build under the outside ski. As they gain experience, skiers can adopt a narrower and narrower stance because they can better anticipate the centrifugal force and thus assess the direction of the resultant and the balance axis.

EXERCISE As is often the case with athletic skills, when it comes to estimating centrifugal force and how to balance against it, experience is the best teacher. The way most skiers get that experience is through making thousands of turns. You can get more useful experience a lot faster if you take the time to do some simple exercises, described here and shown in figure 9.1. They are appropriate for anyone who can make a parallel turn.

- Ski on one ski (figure 9.1*a*). Hold one ski off the snow and make five or six turns on the other. Then switch feet.
- Make turns on the inside ski of each turn, holding your outside ski off the snow.
- Reuele Christies (pronounced "royal"). Once you can turn comfortably on your inside ski, lean forward and hold your outside ski up behind you (figure 9.1*b*).
- Rhythm change-ups. Make four shallow turns at the same rhythm that let you build up a little speed, then make as sharp a turn as you can. Repeat.
- Stopping short. On a gentle slope, go straight down the hill for a bit, then pivot your skis sideways and stop in as short a distance as you can.
- Linked turns on a sidehill. On a moderate to steep slope with no traffic, make linked turns going across the hill rather than down the fall line, so that the turns are asymmetric with regard to the fall line.

a

b

FIGURE 9.1   Exercises to develop lateral balance skills: *(a)* skiing on one ski, and *(b)* reuele Christies. Skiers: *(a)* Phil Mahre; *(b)* Rick Rauch.

Balancing on the Inside and Outside Ski

One of the most important fundamental skills of skiing is balancing predominantly on the outside ski, to the tune of 90 to 100 percent, while turning. For many skiers this skill doesn't come naturally, especially when the situation is intimidating, so this is a skill that deserves particular attention.

Ever since the arrival of shaped skis, however, much attention has been given to the way the best competitive skiers use their inside ski during a turn. Prior to shaped skis, their lateral balance was very outside-dominant, as they balanced virtually their full weight over the outside ski in nearly every turn (soft snow and flats were the common exceptions). To hold a tight turn on hard snow, they simply had to put all the pressure they could muster on the outside ski.

Modern shaped skis have made it possible to use the inside ski in ways we seldom could before, primarily because making the outside ski bend into reverse camber and shape a turn, especially a carved one, doesn't require us to put all our weight on it. It's important to understand, however, that the inside and outside skis are often most useful when used for separate functions; trying to do the same thing with both of them all the time is a limiting approach to skiing.

How can you tell how much weight a skier has on the inside ski if it's on the snow? The best indicator is the amount of snow that's coming out from under it compared to the outside ski. Whether the ski leaves a track in the snow or is bent into reverse camber doesn't tell you much. Just 10 percent of the skier's weight applied to the inside ski is enough to make it bend into reverse camber and leave a track in the snow, meaning fully 90 percent of the skier's weight is on the outside ski.

The Importance of Using the Outside Ski

As long as I can remember, ever since I began skiing in the mid-1950s, instructors and coaches have exhorted their charges to "Stand on your downhill ski!" (And I'm sure they were saying it for decades before that.) When turning, that advice translates to "Stand on your outside ski!" (figure 9.2).

FIGURE 9.2 When the going gets tough, the tough stand on the outside ski. Marco Buechel of Liechtenstein focuses his weight on the outside ski to hold his line in this high-speed fall-away turn on the rock-hard snow of Beaver Creek's Birds of Prey downhill course.

Patrick Russel, one of the best slalom and giant slalom racers of the early 1970s, said that the most important tip he could give skiers was to work constantly from outside foot to outside foot. Marc Girardelli, the only skier to win the overall World Cup five times, and certainly one of the best skiers to ever slide down the hill, has said that once you can balance perfectly on the outside ski, everything else follows.

Since the advent of shaped skis and their ability to hold and carve, though, great skiers have become more liberal with their use of the inside ski, making this a common topic of conversation among coaches, instructors, and others interested in technique. But regardless of how a skier uses the inside ski, it's still the outside ski that does the major work of turning the skier. Of the World Cup skiers I have asked, none have claimed that they intentionally put more than 30 to 40 percent of their weight on the inside ski, and most are well below that. Invariably, they still consider the outside ski to be the "working" ski: the one that generates the force from the snow that makes them turn. This view has also been expressed by their coaches.

One of the important benefits of putting your weight on the downhill, or outside, ski is that doing so maximizes your ability to hold and carve on hard snow, as explained in chapter 2. Even when maximizing grip isn't an issue, it pays to put most of your weight on the outside ski because the human body, by its nature, works best when the outside leg is used to support the body against forces from the side, rather than the inside leg. The body's arrangement of bones and muscles is optimized for it. That's why the soccer player in figure 9.3 plants his left foot when he wants to cut to his right. If I were to ask you to jump as far to your left as you could, you would naturally launch yourself off your right foot and land on your left, as shown in figure 9.4. It would feel awkward and unnatural to jump off your left foot and land on your right. Jumping laterally like this is similar in many ways to what you do when you go from one turn to the next, and for the same reasons that you are more powerful and well-balanced jumping from outside foot to outside foot, you turn better when you balance most of your weight on your outside foot.

Standing on the outside foot, the force on a skier is carried by the foot's inside edge, its medial aspect, whose bones are relatively big and arranged in an arch to help carry the load, like an arch supporting a roadway bridge. Standing on the inside foot puts the load on the bones of the foot's little-toe side, its lateral aspect, which lacks those features. There is also a tactical advantage to balancing predominantly on the outside ski: If the outside ski should slip or if you simply overestimate how much inclination is needed for a turn, the inside ski is available for support.

FIGURE 9.3 This soccer player intuitively plants and pushes off his left foot when he wants to cut to his right because it gives him strength, stability, and control.

FIGURE 9.4 A person jumping from side to side naturally lands on and then pushes off from his outside foot.

Benefits of Using the Inside Ski

All other things being equal, putting some weight on the inside ski and actively using the inside leg has real benefits. In most cases, these benefits come from using the inside ski and inside leg for purposes to which they're uniquely suited, rather than trying to make the inside ski do the same thing as the outside ski. As coaches and competitors have expressed to me, you use the inside ski so that the outside ski works better.

Stabilizing and Supporting the Hips. Putting some force, as little as 5 to 10 percent of your weight, on the inside ski significantly stabilizes the hips in all directions, enabling you to control the outside ski and the force against it with much more precision and finesse. You can demonstrate this to yourself with a simple exercise. While balancing on one foot and holding the other off the ground, try making some typical skiing movements. Move up and down and forward and back. Pretend you're edging your ski with your knee and then flattening it. Next, put your other foot lightly on the ground and repeat those movements. You should immediately feel that you have more control.

Pressure on the inside ski also helps with hip alignment and angulation. As described in chapter 4, hip angulation, which balances the center of gravity over the head of the outside femur, requires that the pelvis be tilted toward the outside when viewed in the frontal plane. Supporting the inside half of the pelvis with the inside leg can help control that alignment.

Support Going Into the Fall Line. A common use of the inside ski seen in competition is as a support going into the turn while the skier waits for the right moment to commit to the outside ski. The skier's center of gravity moves toward the inside of the new turn while the new outside ski tracks toward the outside, so that the skier will have sufficient inclination and edge angle when the time comes to carve. During that time, the skier may need some support to keep from falling too far to the inside, and uses the inside ski for that support. In some cases the inside ski may be fairly flat on the snow, so there is little scrubbing or turning effect. Or the skier may edge it to get some turning effect. This move is often used when a skier begins a turn a bit too early or commits a little too far to the inside of the new turn in the transition. Some examples are shown in figure 9.5.

Support in High-Load Carved Turns. Modern skis enable us to carve very sharp turns with great centrifugal forces. Expert skiers will regularly carve turns that require 45 degrees of inclination, subjecting them to 1.4Gs, or total forces 40 percent greater than their body weight. For a skier balanced entirely on the outside ski, that's something like doing a single-leg press of 40 percent of body weight in every turn. World Cup competitors regularly execute turns at 60 to 70 degrees of inclination, subjecting themselves to loads of 2Gs to 3Gs. That's like leg pressing one to two times your weight. Just supporting these kinds of loads on one leg without collapsing is difficult. Controlling the ski's edge angle and the distribution of force fore and aft over the ski while flexing and extending through variations in terrain at the same time, all with precision and finesse, is extremely difficult. Using the inside leg for support is at times essential.

Radius Control. Varying the proportion of the skier's weight that's placed on the inside ski can be used to adjust the radius of the turn. Recall from chapter 2 that the radius that a particular ski can carve is coupled closely to the speed the skier

a

b

FIGURE 9.5 Top-level racers often support themselves partially or completely on the inside ski at the entry to the turn, as *(a)* Hermann Maier of Austria and *(b)* Manfred Moelgg of Italy, the 2008 World Cup slalom title winner, do here.

is going, and that the skier can vary it only a bit, mostly through knee angulation. That analysis is based on the assumption that virtually all of the skier's weight is on the outside ski. If the character of the snow is such that the outside ski can hold with a smaller portion of the skier's weight on it, it's possible that the skier can make the outside ski carve a tighter arc by shifting balance toward the inside ski. That's because as the skier's center of gravity goes farther to the inside of the turn, putting more weight on the inside ski, the outside ski's edge angle increases. Greater edge angle means deeper reverse camber (figure 2.11*a*, p. 26), and deeper reverse camber means a smaller carving radius.

Two things are important to understand, however. First, the outside ski is still doing the carving. The inside ski will not be able to carve a functional arc because its edge angle will be significantly lower than the outside ski's. Second, there must be enough force on the ski perpendicular to the snow's surface to make the ski penetrate and hold (figure 2.4, p. 21). If you make a turn in a tuck by sliding one foot out to the side to get it on edge while keeping half your weight on a flatter inside ski, these are the mechanics you're using. They can be used in many turns. An example is the start of the turn Lindsey Vonn makes in figure 4.19 on page 68.

FIGURE 9.6   Ivica Kostelic steers his inside ski into the upcoming turn. This is an example of a trigger mechanism some skiers find useful.

Trigger Mechanism.   Some experts and competitors describe actively turning the inside leg at the start of the turn as a useful technique, as Ivica Kostelic does in figure 9.6. The beneficial effect is probably not that this turns the inside ski but rather that it triggers a chain of movements that helps the skier establish proper inclination, edge angles, and forward pressure early in the turn.

The Importance of Hand and Arm Position

One of the most common technical errors in skiing is dropping the inside hand, which pulls the skier's balance away from the outside ski. Another common problem, raising the outside hand, usually has the same effect. Watch the inside hands of World Cup skiers, particularly in the toughest turns. The inside hand is at least as high as the outside hand, and reaching in the same direction. The best skiers in the world strive for quiet, level arms (figure 9.7). Those whose arm discipline is less than perfect usually admit that they would ski better if their arms didn't move around so much. And quiet arms don't come naturally. Limiting arm movement is part of the basic training of all great skiers, who at some point in their lives have done countless drills to develop quiet, balanced hands.

Try to keep your inside hand in your field of view at all times. If it's in view, you know it's at least in the ballpark of proper positioning. Better still, work to keep both hands at the same level, with forearms parallel to the snow. Avoid the common problem of reaching forward with your downhill hand to plant your pole while your inside hand drops. Doing so pulls your downhill shoulder and hip forward, flattening your outside ski. If your hands are always up, level, and in front of you, you'll hardly have to move your downhill hand to plant your pole in the right place at the right time.

EXERCISE   To help develop solid, quiet arms, try this exercise: Tie a 5-foot (1.5 m) piece of string into a loop. Put your hands in the loop, hold them far enough apart to keep the loop snug, and go skiing (figure 9.8). The loop helps keep your hands where you want them and prevents you from dropping one or the other. A few runs like this every now and then will significantly improve your arm discipline and your lateral balance.

FIGURE 9.7 Marlies Schild of Austria keeps her hands level and well in front of her, aiding her lateral balance. Schild is second only to Janica Kostelic in her consistency and dominance of World Cup slalom in the past decade. Her great technique differs from Kostelic's, particularly in the way she angulates, primarily due to physiological differences.

FIGURE 9.8 Skiing with a loop of string around your hands is an excellent way to develop quiet, level arms. Skier: Carol Levine.

Linking Turns: The Challenge of the Transition

When you make the transition from one turn to another, centrifugal force changes directions. Consequently, when you make a turn to the left, your center of gravity must be to the inside of your right foot, and when you make a turn to the right, your center of gravity must be to the inside of your left foot (figure 9.9). Skiing in a wedge or a wide parallel stance makes this simple because your center of gravity is always to the inside of one of your feet. But accomplishing it in a hip-width or narrower parallel stance is much more difficult. This is because your center of gravity must be to the inside of both feet in every turn, and getting the center of gravity to switch sides with both feet in a continuous fluid movement requires you to exercise advanced judgment and techniques and, as we'll see shortly, demands that you actually put yourself out of balance and execute what amounts to be a controlled fall down the hill. Acquiring this skill, called *crossover* by instructors, is the watershed at which advanced skiing begins.

FIGURE 9.9 The skier must be inclined toward the center of every turn to balance against the lateral force from the snow. As a result, the path of the skier's center of gravity must cross that of the feet during the transition. Skier: Anja Paerson.

The Effect of Ski Design on the Transition

As skis hold tighter turns with greater forces, something significant happens in the transition between linked turns: The angle between the path of the skier's center of gravity and the skier's feet gets greater, and the skier's center of gravity must take a steeper line down the hill as it crosses over the feet (figure 9.10). This makes everything more dynamic and critical in the transition, and has made it a central focus of high-performance technique on modern skis.

The Conventional Progression of Techniques for Linking Turns

Progressing through the skill levels of skiing is, in many ways, a matter of learning more and more sophisticated and difficult ways to manage lateral movement and balance of the center of gravity while linking turns. The conventional learning progression from wedge to stem and ultimately to parallel turns, which has been an essential part of the ski instruction canon since the 1920s, addresses the challenge of learning to balance laterally and manage the lateral motion of the center of gravity when going from one turn to the next (figure 9.11).

When people first learn to ski, they make turns in a wedge, which enables them to link turns without their centers of gravity ever having to cross the paths of their feet (figure 9.12 on p. 146).

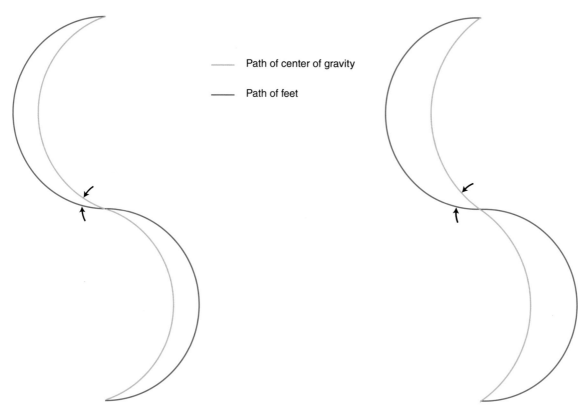

FIGURE 9.10 The more radically turns are carved and the more the skier inclines into the turn, the greater the angle between the paths of the skier's center of gravity and feet as they cross in the transition.

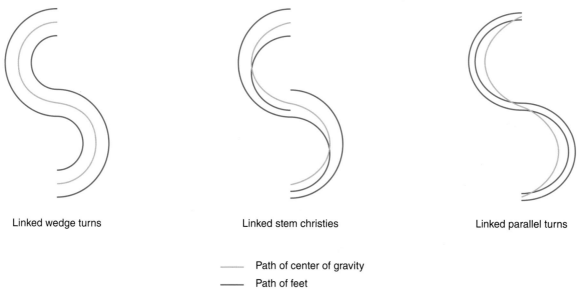

Linked wedge turns   Linked stem christies   Linked parallel turns

—— Path of center of gravity
—— Path of feet

FIGURE 9.11 The paths of the skier's center of gravity and feet in various types of turns shows how refined the skier's lateral balance must be to make each one.

FIGURE 9.12   A wedge makes lateral balance easy: The skier's center of gravity never has to cross the path of either foot when going from turn to turn. Skier: Cait Boyd.

The next step in learning to link turns and the simplest way to accomplish the crossover between your feet and your center of gravity is to step the new outside ski outward at the start of the new turn, as shown in figure 9.13. This is called an *uphill stem* (from the German *stemmen,* "to push against"), which safely and securely establishes both a steering angle and the inward lean relative to the outside ski of the new turn.

After having learned this movement, many skiers spend the rest of their skiing careers trying to avoid it. It's the stem turn initiation for which so many otherwise good skiers chastise themselves, wishing they could "ski parallel." And some instructors contend that skiers should never learn to turn this way in the first place—that there are other ways to learn to ski that will never require skiers to make a stem turn. It's as if they all see the stem turn as a Venus flytrap technique that, once learned, forever holds a skier in its clutches.

It's true that some skiers can learn to make parallel turns without first learning to make stem turns, or even wedge turns. But there are many who can't, and there's nothing wrong with learning to turn with an uphill stem. The reason intermediate skiers get stuck in this technique is that they don't properly learn other, more advanced techniques, the first of which is a more advanced form of the stem move: one in which the stem is combined with a movement of the center of gravity across

a

b

FIGURE 9.13 By extending the uphill ski in a stem, the skier establishes both an initial steering angle and an inclined relation between her center of gravity and new outside ski while being supported by the downhill ski. *(a)* This recreational skier keeps her center of gravity tracking with her downhill foot as she stems her uphill ski. *(b)* Spaniard Maria Jose Rienda also stems her uphill ski as she initiates this turn while on her way to winning a World Cup giant slalom in Aspen, Colorado. In contrast to the skier in figure *a*, Rienda's center of gravity is moving laterally across her downhill foot as she stems the uphill ski. This is a more advanced, and desirable, form of stem turn.

the feet (figure 9.13*b*). This is an essential and useful technique that the best skiers in the world use regularly.

To progress beyond the intermediate-level stem, you've got to move beyond distinctly separate turns and learn to meld the completion of one turn with the initiation of the next in a single, continuous transition phase. The key to linking turns this way is getting your center of gravity to change sides with your feet by using the dynamics of the end of one turn to help you start the next one. To put it more concretely, you must learn how to go out of balance in a deliberate and precisely controlled fashion as you near the end of one turn, and then catch yourself smoothly in the control phase the next.

FIGURE 9.14   To link parallel turns, both the skier's feet must swap sides with his center of gravity at the same time. Skier: David N. Oliver.

Falling Into the Turn

Learning to smoothly link parallel turns, as shown in figure 9.14, is similar, in an important way, to learning to walk: Both movements involve committing to a period of imbalance. Toddlers take their first unaided steps by falling forward, then catching themselves with an outstretched foot. That's how we all learned to walk. Eventually, the movements come smoothly, and the moment of imbalance is imperceptible. Still, every step we make for the rest of our lives begins with a controlled fall.

To begin a parallel turn from a narrow stance, you must also learn to make a controlled fall. The toddler falls forward, anticipating the floor's support of the outstretched foot. You fall diagonally toward the center of the new turn, anticipating the centrifugal force of the turn and the lateral force from the snow that will support you once the skis have engaged the snow.

Going into a traverse between turns is like bringing your feet together and standing still between steps as you walk. Each turn and each step is separated by a period of static balance. Fluid movement begins when you move continuously and directly from one step to the next, and from one turn to the next. Good skiing, whether it's in moguls, broken snow, or a slalom course, isn't a succession of individual turns—disjoint curves joined by lines and angles—but rather a smooth thread of arcs that flow each into the next with no discernable break.

You must (and this is the hardest part) let yourself go out of balance and topple from the old turn, across your skis and down the hill, toward the center of the new turn. How fast and in exactly what direction you let yourself fall is dictated by a host of factors that only experience can teach you to recognize and evaluate.

This whole business is scary for skiers learning to make parallel turns. Being out of balance is something they've worked hard to avoid. For skiers who have the judgment to know how much centrifugal force awaits them and when it will come, this period of premeditated imbalance is the source of one of skiing's great sensations: the weightless feeling of flying into the turn.

Skiing becomes much more interesting and fun when you begin to add a dynamic transition with a period of imbalance to your turns. It's the gateway to high-performance skiing, and remains a key point of focus for expert skiers and racers throughout their skiing careers.

Estimating the Transition

As just explained, walking involves falling forward with every step and landing on your outstretched foot. Running is a bit more advanced, but much the same. With each stride, you estimate where to put your foot next so that you land in balance with the right momentum to carry you forward into the next stride. Imagine a similar but even more advanced activity: running along a mountain trail or stream bed, jumping from rock to rock, looking ahead, and quickly estimating how hard to jump and in just which direction to hit the next good landing spot.

a

b

FIGURE 9.15 By the second frame of figure *a* (and probably before that), Martina Ertl of Germany knows where she wants to start carving in the next turn. From the third through the seventh frames, she is toppling across her skis. She lands in the eighth frame with about the right amount of inclination, forward pressure, and initial steering angle to begin carving the next turn, although she may be a bit too far inside. American Sarah Schleper, in figure *b*, overestimates how far into the turn she should topple and ends up much farther to the inside when her skis finally engage the snow.

This sort of estimation problem is what you're faced with when you make dynamic parallel turns. Once you start the transition and your body begins toppling toward the inside of the next turn, you have little control over its motion. So you have to enter the transition with things pretty well planned out so that you come down on your skis in the right place at the right time, with the right inclination, the right fore–aft balance, the right angulation, and the right initial steering angle (figure 9.15).

FIGURE 9.16   The space between the first two turns allows Janica Kostelic to extend in the transition between them. The shorter distance between the second and third turns, and the fact that the second turn comes so far out of the fall line, requires her to flex in the transition so that she doesn't overshoot the entry to the third turn.

That's a lot to get right. Hitting the mark requires knowing ahead of time how the snow will respond to your skis and your momentum, how long it will take before you build enough pressure under your skis to make them bite, and innumerable other factors that only the mountain and the snow can teach you through making innumerable turns.

Let me emphasize: You must make your estimate *before* you start your transition. You need to look into the next turn and decide just where you want your body to go, and then make it go there. Misestimating the target in the upcoming turn, or not making the correct movements to take them there, might be the most common error that keeps good skiers from being great skiers.

This estimation problem is closely related to questions of unweighting. How you deal with the virtual bump, whether you up-unweight, down-unweight, and how much, depends on how far it is from the beginning of the transition to the control phase of the next turn and how fast you're going. You can't get any real turning done during the transition. So if you want to get into the next turn quickly, you need to keep the transition short by absorbing the virtual bump. If you've got some space, you can extend and be light and loose on the snow for a bit. This has the advantage of letting your hard-working muscles relax for a moment and flush lactate and of allowing you to extend and take a deep breath. The choice is driven by where you want the engagement point of your next turn—the start of its control phase—to be (figure 9.16).

Techniques for Transitions

There are many good techniques for executing a crossover, that is, getting your center of gravity and feet to swap sides. An expert skier will use all the ones described here in the course of a day of skiing. A single turn often incorporates several. Knowing them all, and blending them to suit the situation at hand, is a hallmark of good skiing.

Making the Feet Slow Down or Turn More Sharply. Any action that makes your feet slow down in relation to your upper body can be used to produce a crossover (figure 9.17). When you finish a turn against a mogul, for example, your feet slow down, the rest of your body keeps going, and they swap sides.

Other examples abound. A sharp edgeset at the end of a turn sets the same mechanism in motion. Another example is the *preturn*, a maneuver commonly taught in ski schools in the 1950s, '60s, and '70s, and still used today. In preparation for a turn from a traverse, the skier first makes a small, sharp turn up the hill. Momentum carries the body across the skis toward the center of the upcoming turn. Look closely at the skiers around you, and you'll see this maneuver in many turns.

Making the feet slow down is also one of the main purposes of the downhill stem that many skiers make between turns. The stem is sort of a one-ski preturn, retarding the skier's downhill foot while the skier's body keeps going.

A preturn can cause a crossover without making the feet slow down, too, if it's carved. At the end of the turn the skis are forced to turn more sharply, with a bit of forward pressure, a bit more angulation, or a bit more of both. Your upper body, traveling on a broader arc, then passes over your feet toward the inside of the next turn. Look closely at Manuela Moelgg in the fifth frame of figure 9.18, and you'll

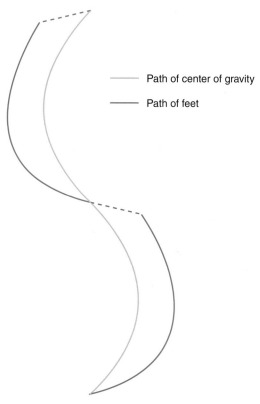

Path of center of gravity
Path of feet

FIGURE 9.17 By making the feet slow down or turn more sharply at the end of the turn than your upper body, you can make your center of gravity cross over your feet.

FIGURE 9.18 By increasing her knee angulation in the fifth frame, Manuela Moelgg of Italy starts her transition to the next turn.

see that she has turned her left knee in a bit. This makes her ski turn slightly more sharply, which puts her a bit out of balance to the outside, making her topple across her skis into the next turn. Martina Ertl does the same thing in the third frame of figure 9.15*a* on page 149.

FIGURE 9.19 In the second frame, German racer Alois Vogl has lifted his right ski from the snow and begins to topple to his right, toward the center of the next turn. This establishes the inward lean he'll need when the new outside ski engages the snow in the sixth frame.

Removing the Support of the Downhill Ski. Imagine you're skiing across the hill with most of your weight on your downhill foot. What happens if you simply pick up your downhill foot? You fall down the hill. This is the basis of an essential technique, seen most often in medium turns but also used in short turns. From a position of balance at the end of the turn with most of your weight on the downhill ski, you stand on your uphill ski and either lift your downhill ski (figure 9.19) or relax the downhill leg. As your center of gravity falls into the new turn, the new outside ski, the one to which you just stepped, rolls onto its inside edge. As the ski changes edges, you twist it to the initial steering angle you need for the new turn.

Flexing. The techniques of passive and active flexion (discussed in chapter 6), when executed during the completion phase of the turn, cause the path of the center of gravity to cross over that of the feet. During the completion phase of the turn, you quickly flex at the knees and waist by relaxing your thigh, buttock, and lower-back muscles, and possibly contracting your hip flexors. At this moment the snow is no longer pushing on your body from the thighs up. With no external force from the snow acting on the majority of your body, it no longer follows a curved path. Its momentum carries it in a straight line. Because your skis still have contact with the snow, however, they'll continue to turn, carrying your feet with them. As a result, your body moves across your feet to start the new turn while your feet pass underneath, finishing the old one (figure 9.20).

At the moment you flex, you immediately feel released from the old turn. Your body flies across your feet into the new turn and feels as if it's accelerating, although it really isn't. When executed properly, you'll feel like your upper body is starting the new turn while your feet finish the old one.

With each new generation of skis we're able to make tighter and more aggressively carved turns, which require more inclination throughout each turn. These turns produce larger virtual bumps, requiring a greater range of extension and flexion. For these reasons, the importance of flexion in the transition and extension into the fall line has increased steadily over the years to the point that they're now essential techniques for all skiers who carve turns.

Lateral Support From the Pole Plant. When advanced skiers are faced with challenging situations, they often lose the confidence to commit their centers of gravity into the turn ahead of their feet. It is, after all, committing to being out of balance, albeit briefly. Instead, they often adopt the safe alternative of an uphill stem while staying balanced firmly on the downhill ski. Another common, but worse, alternative

a

b

FIGURE 9.20　Flexing to initiate the transition works in turns of all sizes. In figure *a*, Massimiliano Blardone of Italy uses the technique for two giant slalom turns, and in figure *b*, World Cup athlete Chemmy Alcott of Great Britain makes a quick transition between two slalom-size turns by flexing.

Mario Matt

Contrary to what you might expect, shaped skis did not catch on right away on the World Cup. Although they were widely accepted by the ski instruction community by 1999, no serious contenders in the World Championship slalom that year were on them. The conventional wisdom among the established stars was that the new short, shaped skis were OK on easy terrain and soft snow, but weren't up to the demands of steep hills and hard snow. That all changed the next December when Finn Christian Jagge, a seasoned veteran, decided to give the new skis a try and notched a surprise victory in the World Cup slalom at Madonna di Campiglio, a demanding hill with a very steep pitch. The new skis were suddenly legitimized, and everyone started scrambling to figure them out.

As the old-guard slalom elite were adjusting to the new gear, Mario Matt hit the World Cup. A young man who clearly understood the new skis, Matt won the second World Cup race he was ever in, at Kitzbühel, Austria. He went on to win the slalom at Schladming, Austria, that season and landed on the podium a total of four times—an auspicious debut.

His line and technique were distinctly different. The conventional technique usually involved going into the turn light, then punching hard in a short, dramatic control phase near the pole. In contrast, Matt hugged the snow in the transition by flexing and often actively retracting, enabling him to edge and pressure his skis earlier in the turn than everyone else. That and his wide stance in the transition gave him more edge angle and inclination, too. The result was that Matt had shorter transitions and longer control phases that were better carved. Many described the resulting line as something akin to very small giant slalom turns.

Matt has continued to be at the forefront of slalom racing. He has won races in all but one of his 10 years on the World Cup, and has taken the World Championship slalom crown twice. (The only other male skier in the modern era to win the slalom World Championship more than once is Ingemar Stenmark.)

Matt's skiing is precise and controlled. As with many of the best skiers, his hands are always in the same place: well in front of his body and level with each other. When you see him ski, you see someone who is clearly skiing with his feet, getting every iota of performance from his cutting-edge skis.

is to quickly pivot the skis and thrust them to the side, sometimes with upper-body rotation. This quickly generates lateral force against which the skier can balance. Neither solution is a good one.

Once you've allowed your body's momentum to carry you across the skis and into the new turn, there's only one way you can control your body's lateral motion until your skis engage the snow in the next turn: a pole planted in the snow. That's why skiers who have weak or unreliable pole plants have trouble on steep, challenging terrain and start most of their turns with an uphill stem.

The support of a properly planted pole allows you to commit fully to the turn without worrying about overcommitting. If you let yourself go a bit too far toward the center of the new turn, the pole will be there for support. This requires that you plant the pole solidly, with a firm grip, and at the very beginning of the turn (figure 9.21).

FIGURE 9.21 In turns on a steep slope, a solid, reliable pole plant enables the skier to commit to a strong crossover by providing lateral support. Skier: Charley Stocker.

Often, when initiating very short turns on a steep slope, accomplished skiers will quickly get the upper body across the feet and into the new turn, and suspend it there with the pole while pivoting their unweighted skis through the fall line. With the skis off the snow and the pole planted firmly at the proper angle, as described in chapter 7, the skier can pivot the skis 180 degrees if need be. This is an essential technique on extremely steep terrain (see figure 14.5, p. 204).

Choosing Your Weapon. When you come down to it, there's seldom a single best technique for getting your body to go across your feet between any two given turns. Two expert skiers will often use two different approaches in the same situation, as in figure 3.21 (p. 50), in which Benjamin Raich extends and Massimiliano Blardone flexes. And as with techniques for turning the skis, skiers might mix several of the techniques we've discussed in this chapter in a single turn, such as tightening the old turn and making a slight uphill stem. The best skiers have a lot of tools in their kit, and being able to combine them on the fly gives their skiing a spontaneous, improvisational flavor that sets them apart.

CHAPTER 10

Boots

It's easy to get excited about skis. New designs appear every year, looking cooler than the old ones, and you talk about them with your friends on the chair lift and over beers. By comparison, boots are dull. They don't change much from year to year, or even from decade to decade. You talk about them with your boot fitter the way you might talk with an orthopedic surgeon about your knees.

There's no question, however, that your boots have a more significant effect on the quality of your skiing than do your skis or any other piece of equipment. The pros I know would rather have an airline lose their skis than their boots—that should tell you something. So although it can take some time to pick the right pair, set them up, and tweak them as close to perfection as you can, doing so is worth the effort. It's simply wrong to think that the best you can expect is a compromise between performance and comfort.

If you want to ski your best, you owe it to yourself to experiment with your boots, and to get a new pair now and then. (Although you can hardly tell from trying them on in the shop, boot designs do improve from year to year.) Skiers who believe their boots are just fine because they're comfortable and ski pretty well are missing the boat. In this chapter we'll talk about facets of boot design and setup that will help you approach ski boot nirvana. Some features are built into the boot and can't be changed, some you can experiment with on your own, and some require the tools and expertise of a good boot fitter.

The Boot Is Part of the Ski

Once your boot is in the binding, it's effectively part of the ski. It's not a hiking boot on steroids, it's your ski's handle—a lever you control with your leg and foot. You work the ski by working the handle, pushing against one part of the boot or another. To control the edge of the ski, you push with your leg against the side of the boot. To adjust how pressure is distributed along the ski's length, you push against the front or back. Figures 10.1 and 10.2 show some examples. When we watch great skiers ski, our eyes tend to be drawn to other parts of their bodies, so these movements are easy to miss. But when you see someone making great turns, look at the feet: That's where much of the action is.

FIGURE 10.1   The boot is the handle through which you work the ski. In the third frame, Mario Matt edges his outside ski by pushing with his leg against the side of his boot. Then, going into the next turn in the fifth frame, he presses his left shin into the inside front corner of his left boot cuff to make the ski bite and turn.

FIGURE 10.2   Aksel Lund Svindal uses the back of his boot to shift pressure to the tail of his outside ski, helping release it from the turn.

Getting Boots Right

If we compared a skier to a sports car, we'd say that the skier's upper body is the car's body and chassis, the skis are the wheels, and the legs and boots are the suspension and steering components that connect the wheels to the chassis. A car won't handle properly if the suspension and steering components aren't set up and aligned properly, and the same is true for a skier. Your boots determine the mechanical relation between your skis and your body and provide the surfaces you push on with your feet and legs to control your skis (figure 10.3). An everyday passenger car will drive acceptably if you take it to the local tire shop, have the mechanics put it on the alignment rack, and dial it in to spec. But for a race car to be competitive, its suspension must be tweaked and tuned to provide just the right handling. Similarly, a recreational skier's boots will perform adequately if they're bought from a good boot fitter who matches the right make and model to the skier and does some rudimentary setup work. But if you're serious about this sport and want to ski your best, you've got to put some time into tweaking and tuning your boots.

Finding a good boot fitter is part of the process. Ask instructors for recommendations. If there's a race club in your area or where you ski, ask the coaches. The more references you can get, the better. Whoever you go with, expect a guaranteed fit. Be wary of someone who wants to do a lot of work on your boots all at once. This isn't like getting a suit altered. It should be iterative. And if you're less than happy, find someone else.

Of course your boots must be pain free and comfortable. You can't ski well otherwise. But you can't stop there, as too many skiers do. You need to take the next step and adjust subtle but important aspects of the fit and parameters of the shell geometry. You can take that step on your own, but you'll be ahead of the game if you team up with a skilled boot fitter. A good one will get you in the right boot to begin with, which is the most important step in getting your boots right. A *really* good boot fitter will know if the best boot for you is one the shop doesn't sell, and will tell you what it is and maybe where to find it. You should go buy those boots, then bring them back to that boot fitter to work with you through the rest of the process.

A special note about buying boots for adolescents: Always buy boots that fit them *now.* Don't buy boots to grow into. Boots that are too big are a huge roadblock to learning to ski well: The right movements don't work, so the skier learns another way to ski. By the time the boots fit, the bad movements are ingrained, which makes it doubly hard for the skier to learn the right ones.

FIGURE 10.3 The boot is a lever you use to control the ski. The parts of the boot that provide the most control are shown here. These are the places where it's most important that your boots fit well.

Stiffness

When it comes to lateral stiffness, a lot is good, and more is usually better, although it's not always necessary. Frontal stiffness, which I'll simply call "stiffness" from here on, is more complicated.

It's easy to be tempted into buying boots that are too stiff in the front. That's because the hotter the model, the stiffer the boot, and most of us want to be hot. If the stiffness is adjustable, fine. If it's not, beware. And keep in mind that ski boots are stiffer outside in the cold than they are in the ski shop. Ideally, the front of the boot's cuff should fit close to the shin and get progressively stiffer as the boot is flexed. The cuff should never feel like a hard wall that your shin runs into when you flex your ankle. Younger skiers, especially, should avoid boots that are too stiff and limit the use of their ankles. They don't have the mass needed to flex a stiff boot, but more important, they ski better and develop better technically in boots that allow more range of motion in the ankle than that provided by some high-performance boots targeted at skiers their age.

Having said all that, it's easier for a good boot fitter to soften a boot that's too stiff in the front than it is to stiffen one that's too soft, so when in doubt, go a little stiffer (without going overboard). To find the right forward flex, you'll want to consider your personal body type, the type of skiing you want to do, and your skiing ability.

Your Personal Body Type. In general, the bigger the skier, the stiffer the boot. If you carry relatively more mass around your hips than in your upper torso, consider a softer boot because this physique makes forward lean adjustment critical—and difficult (see Forward Lean, p. 164). Slim hips and broad shoulders allow more options. If you're tall with long legs, you might do well with a stiffer boot. You should know that stiffness of a particular model from a particular manufacturer often varies with size. One cuff size will typically be used for up to several boot sizes, and smaller boot sizes tend to be stiffer than bigger sizes.

The Type of Skiing You Want to Do. If you spend your time cruising, skiing fast, skiing in very soft snow, or skiing in big moguls, a softer forward flex will work better for you. Many ski racers use softer boots for downhill than for slalom and giant slalom, and many mogul competitors ski in softer-flexing boots.

If you ski mostly on hard snow or love making short, quick turns, more beef in the front of the boot is helpful. Boots that are stiff in the front facilitate these sorts of turns but require technical finesse. The performance boost they give you on hard, smooth snow may or may not be worth the difficulties they present in other conditions, especially moguls.

Your Skiing Ability. Unless you're a true expert with the experience to know just what you like, steer clear of the stiffest racing boots on the rack. You'll probably ski better in something softer. Then again, a boot that's mushy in the front or well below your ability level is just as bad, especially on hard snow.

Conventional high-performance ski boots depend on an arcane, and some would say archaic, mechanism to control their frontal stiffness: the deformation of the boot itself. When the skier's leg pushes into the front of the cuff, the cuff deforms a bit. Looking down on the boot from above, it becomes less circular and more oval. Just as important, the cuff mashes down on the lower shell over the instep and, depending on the boot's design, might also pull forward on the rear spine of the lower shell. Buckling the boot tighter makes it stiffer by making the shell harder to deform. The shell's resistance to deformation is what makes a race boot ski the way it does and, unfortunately, makes it so hard to get your foot in and out of.

Ski boot tongues are stiff, too, and can be used to fine-tune the boot's overall stiffness. Snugging up the boot's power strap on the tongue rather than the shell, as shown in figure 10.4, gives you a flex control that relies on compressing and deforming the tongue rather than the shell and gives the boot a more progressive flex than when you put the strap on the outside of the shell. The elastic Booster strap, available as a replacement for conventional power straps and popular among expert skiers and racers at the highest levels, provides further refinement in controlling the boot's forward flex. Rather than relying on the tongue's resistance to compression or bending to control flex, the strap itself stretches under load, providing resistance that's adjustable on the hill. At least one boot manufacturer is currently fitting a few of its models with a strap based on similar principles.

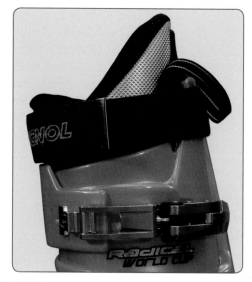

FIGURE 10.4 Putting the power strap against the boot's tongue rather than at the front of the cuff allows a progressive flex from the shell to the tongue.

Footbeds

Practically all the force of a turn pushes through the soles of your feet. It makes sense, then, that your boots should fit the bottoms of your feet at least as well as they fit everywhere else. This is why you should consider having custom footbeds made for your ski boots (figure 10.5). Your boot will fit the bottom of your foot as it should, and your foot and ankle will be prevented from rolling, flattening, and arching excessively as the force increases and decreases under your foot through each turn. You're also likely to find that you get better performance from your boots without having to buckle them as tightly.

a

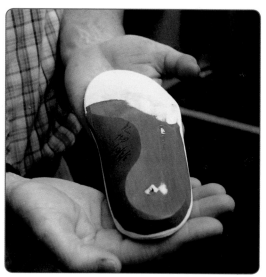

b

FIGURE 10.5 A good pair of custom footbeds will improve both your skiing and your comfort and can last through several pairs of boots. *(a)* Because the footbed's arch precisely conforms to the skier's, the skier is better able to balance against the forces of skiing. *(b)* While the top of this footbed is curved everywhere to match the shape of the skier's foot, the bottom is flat, or *posted* (except under the arch), so that it is stable inside the boot.

Compared to the cost of a pair of boots, custom footbeds aren't expensive, especially considering that a well-fitted and well-made pair will last a long time and can be moved from one pair of boots to another. Just be careful to get them made for you by someone who has a lot of experience. If you have chronic problems with your feet (such as very high arches, hammer toes, or instability), consider having a licensed podiatrist make a pair of true orthotics for your ski boots. Note that although some ski shops talk loosely about making "orthotics" for ski boots, only a podiatrist or certified pedorthist (a specialist licensed or certified, among other things, in making orthotics) can legitimately claim to make them.

Footbeds vary in the firmness of their support and in how much mobility they allow the bones of your feet and ankles as you ski. Some skiers who have very strong and healthy feet prefer to actively control the alignment of their feet and ankles as they ski and want little or no support from the footbed. Bode Miller and others, for example, have won World Cup races with no footbeds to speak of in their boots. Others, like Daron Rahlves, prefer a snug fit and don't want to be able to do anything more than wiggle their toes a bit. Most skiers do best with at least a moderate amount of support under their feet.

There aren't any hard and fast answers to the question of how firm and supportive a pair of footbeds should be. It's largely a matter of personal taste. A good boot fitter is your best ally here. These are among the factors that determine how much support your footbeds will give you:

- The material the footbeds are made from.
- The amount of pressure on your foot when the footbeds are molded. Most footbeds are molded when you're sitting and your feet are either hanging free or supporting the weight they normally would when you're sitting on the edge of a chair. Footbeds should be molded in a standing position only if you're standing on a special device (designed for the purpose) that supports your arch from below.
- Whether or not the footbeds are posted. A posted footbed is flat on the bottom under the heel, so it can't roll in the boot (figure 10.5b). Most skiers do best with posted footbeds.

When your ankle flexes forward in a ski boot, your knee might not go straight forward. A little variance from straight ahead is acceptable, but it's worth getting it close to straight. For most people, the knee will go inward (figure 10.6), although some people's go outward. The ankle, normally a complicated joint, is essentially reduced to a simple hinge when it's in a ski boot. If the axis of that hinge were perfectly oriented, lying entirely in the frontal plane and parallel to the sole of your boot, the knee would go straight forward when the ankle closes (called *dorsiflexion*). But the axis is usually quite a few degrees off from that, and the boot may not flex that way either, which is why the knee might not track straight.

a   b

FIGURE 10.6 Some people's knees go inward when their ankles dorsiflex, whereas others' knees go outward. This person's knees go inward slightly. By adjusting the tilt of the footbeds in the frontal plane, your knees can be made to track straight. You can make the adjustment with a strip of rubber or plastic taped to the bottom of the footbed or to the top of the boot's bootboard.

For most people, tilting the footbed outward or inward by a few degrees will adequately adjust the alignment of the ankle's hinging axis. The simplest way to do this is to build up strips of tape or tape a strip of firm material under one edge of the footbed. Putting them under the inside edge and giving the footbed *varus* tilt will help correct an inward movement of the knee; putting them under the outside edge, giving the footbed *valgus* tilt, will help bring the knee in if it's going outward when the ankle flexes.

Custom footbeds are an important part of the boot-tuning package for most performance-oriented skiers. But perfect boot setup can't be achieved with only custom footbeds and the adjustments you can make to them. These work in conjunction with the two principle angles of the boot itself: forward lean and lateral cant, which we'll discuss next. To ski your best, these parameters must be addressed too.

Forward Lean

As mentioned in chapter 4 in the Lower-Leg Angle section, the purpose of *forward lean* in the boot's cuff, shown in figure 10.7, is to allow the skier to move through a long range of vertical motion without affecting balance fore and aft. Having the right amount of forward lean is crucial to good skiing, especially in moguls and racing. You should check it every time you try on a new pair of boots using a simple procedure we'll describe soon, and set it up properly for the boots you have. How much forward lean a skier needs is specific to the skier's body type. In particular, it depends on the relative lengths of the skier's femur and torso, the relative distribution of mass in the upper legs, hips, and torso, and the shape of the calf muscle. A long femur tends to make the skier's center of gravity go backward as the skier flexes. So, too, will above-average mass in the thighs and hips. A long torso and mass in the chest and shoulders tend to bring the center of gravity forward. A thick calf muscle tilts the lower leg forward, and a thin calf muscle stands it up straighter.

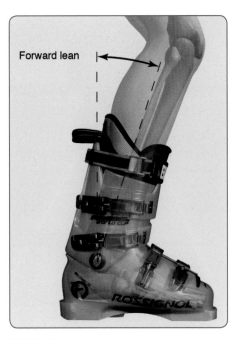

FIGURE 10.7 A boot's forward lean is the angle, in the sagittal plane, between the midline of its cuff and a vertical line. The right amount for an individual is determined by that person's physical characteristics, not skiing ability. It's important that you have the right amount for *you*.

EXERCISE   Fortunately, a simple test, shown in figure 10.8, can tell you if your boots' forward lean is appropriate for you. Buckle your boots up tight and find a hard, level floor. The top buckle in particular must be as tight as it would be for aggressive skiing. Now see how low you can crouch before you lose your balance backward. Be sure to keep your hands out in front of you at shoulder level, reaching as far forward as possible. You should be able to flex as low as the skier in figure 10.8a, with your femurs parallel to the ground, and still be comfortably in balance fore and aft. If you can't get that low, your boots need more forward lean. If you can get a lot lower than that, you might have more lean than you really need. Also try the test with lifts under your heels and toes (as shown in figure 10.8, *b-c*) to see how differences in forward lean affect your balance. The critical factor that changes in these tests is the angle of your lower legs to the ground. That angle compensates for the restriction your boots place on your ankles' range of motion.

If you can't get your hips level with your knees and still stay balanced over your feet like the skier in figure 10.8a, increase the boots' forward lean until you can. If they have an effective forward lean adjustment, use it. Otherwise, increase the forward lean by inserting some flexible but firm material between the back of

a

b

c

FIGURE 10.8   Crouching as low as he can without falling over backward, this skier shows the effects of his boot's forward lean on his range of vertical movement. With his boots flat on the floor in figure *a*, he can flex to a low stance and remain in balance fore and aft, indicating that his boots have enough forward lean. By putting a cafeteria tray under the toes or heels, he decreases or increases their forward lean by about 4 degrees. With the toes lifted by the tray, in figure *b*, his boot cuffs don't have enough forward lean for him to be in balance in a low stance. With the heels lifted, in figure *c*, he can get very low and still be in good balance fore and aft.

FIGURE 10.9 Forward lean can be increased by inserting trail maps or similar material between the back of the liner and the shell. Shims specifically made for this purpose are also available.

the liner and the boot cuff (figure 10.9). Trail maps, or sheets of rubber or cork, work well for experimenting. Don't be afraid to use a quarter-inch (.6 cm) thickness or more. As with most boot adjustments, you won't know the right amount until you've tried both too little and too much.

Experiment with the setting until you find the spot that works best for you when you're out on the hill skiing. Just make sure you test each setting in situations that demand a long range of vertical motion, such as moguls. Skiers who rarely venture into moguls or who ski in soft boots might be all right with less forward lean than the test suggests. Those who like skiing deep moguls or whose boots are very stiff in the front might want more forward lean than the test suggests. Top-level racers, who have well-developed and relatively massive upper torsos, can generally get as low as or lower than the skier in figure 10.8c.

Once you've settled on how much forward lean you want, visit your boot fitter, who can provide you with boot shims made specifically for this purpose, alter the cuff angle itself, or put plates under the toes or heels of your boots to change the forward lean (figure 10.10). A heel lift inside the boot won't produce the same result. That adjustment addresses a different situation, described later under Heel Lifts.

One last thing to keep in mind: Forward lean angles published by boot manufacturers do not provide meaningful comparisons between brands or models. Different manufacturers measure the angle in different ways, and even within one brand's line, the height of the cuff on different models might make comparisons of their stated forward lean angles meaningless.

Special Considerations for Women

Women typically carry more of their weight in their hips and upper thighs than men do, so their centers of gravity are more apt to move behind their feet as they flex. This suggests that many women might need boots with more forward lean than men. But other factors complicate things. A short lower leg or thick calf muscle will tilt the lower leg forward, effectively increasing the boots' forward lean.

If the shape of your calves pushes your lower legs too far forward or your boots are just too tight around your calves, remove any forward lean shims or other attachments the boots might have. If you still have the problem, try placing a quarter- to half-inch (.6-1.2 cm) heel lift inside each boot. (For test purposes, folded paper napkins or cut-up trail maps placed under the heels of your boot liners work fine.) This will lift the calf muscle farther out of the boot, effectively reducing the boot's forward lean, and at the same time increase your ankle's range of motion. Once your boots fit to your liking around your lower legs, use the test just described to find the right amount of forward lean. All manufacturers have boots in their product lines designed specifically for women. Many of them are quite good, but some focus more on feminine aesthetics than physiology. This is another place where a trustworthy boot fitter is worth driving to the next town for.

a

b

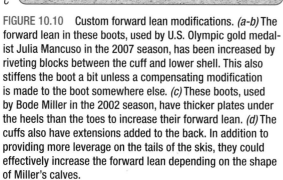

c

d

FIGURE 10.10 Custom forward lean modifications. *(a-b)* The forward lean in these boots, used by U.S. Olympic gold medalist Julia Mancuso in the 2007 season, has been increased by riveting blocks between the cuff and lower shell. This also stiffens the boot a bit unless a compensating modification is made to the boot somewhere else. *(c)* These boots, used by Bode Miller in the 2002 season, have thicker plates under the heels than the toes to increase their forward lean. *(d)* The cuffs also have extensions added to the back. In addition to providing more leverage on the tails of the skis, they could effectively increase the forward lean depending on the shape of Miller's calves.

Lateral Canting

Regardless of how well you angulate and counter, it won't help much if your boots aren't canted properly. The *lateral cant* of a ski boot (or simply *cant*) is the angle, in the frontal plane, of the cuff's midline from a vertical line, as shown in figure 10.11.

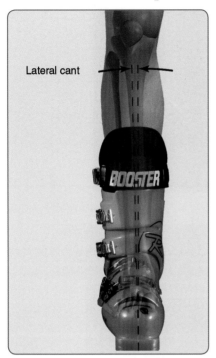

When the cuff is angled outward, the angle is considered positive. Most skiers do well with boots canted between +1 and +3 degrees, but many people require settings outside this range. Boots are rarely set up with negative lateral cant. Anytime you get a new pair of boots, having this parameter checked and set up properly must be part of the package.

Recall that in chapter 4 we saw that when you're inclined into a turn and properly aligned in the frontal plane, a line from your center of mass to the edge of your ski should pass through the head of the femur and the knee, as shown in figure 4.20 on page 69. There are times when you'll adjust the edge and platform angles by moving your knee to one side or the other of that line, but not too far. Proper lateral canting adds another element to that alignment: The middle of the ski will be at a platform angle of 90 degrees, which will make it hold. From there, increased knee angulation will make the ski turn more sharply, and moving the knee outward will make the ski slip. This is a nominal setting. Some skiers like a bit less lateral cant than this and, less commonly, some like a bit more.

By and large, people's legs don't rise straight up from their feet. Most often they bow out slightly. If your legs are shaped like that and your ski boots have no lateral cant, your knee will have to be well inside of the line between your center of

FIGURE 10.11   A boot's lateral cant is the angle between the midline of the cuff and a vertical line when viewed in the frontal plane.

gravity and the edge of your ski to make your ski hold. Canting your boot outward moves the knee into that line.

What if you were to angulate to your physiological limits and the platform angle of your outside ski still exceeded 90 degrees? You would never be able to hold on hard snow. That's the plight of severely undercanted skiers. Try as they might, their skis won't hold because they can't achieve a platform angle of 90 degrees or smaller in the midbody of the ski. Moderately undercanted skiers have problems, too, because they use too much of their range of motion in angulation simply to get the ski to hold, leaving them no ability to tighten the turn by angulating more, and they can't flex the leg at the knee and hip smoothly while making the ski grip. The tails of their skis often slip at the end of the turn, and their excessive knee angulation commonly leaves them facing their tips rather than countering as they go through the turn. Because most skiers naturally push their knee forward as they rotate the leg inward, undercanted skiers also often end up with excessive forward pressure as they go for more and more knee angulation. Such a skier looks knock-kneed much of the time. This is most visible in the bottom half of the turn or when the skier is in a straight run with skis flat on the snow (figure 10.12).

a   *b*

FIGURE 10.12   Undercanted skier: *(a)* in a straight run, and *(b)* in a turn.

An overcanted skier has different problems (figure 10.13). This individual can't make the outside ski slip without taking on a bowlegged stance or pushing the hip out. In the control phase of the turn, a high edge angle and tight platform angle, even when the skier is not highly angulated, make the ski hooky. If severely overcanted, the skier's knee and ankle will be well outside the line of force on the ski all the time, putting a lot of torque on the ankle and making the ski feel choppy and chattery. Overcanted skiers often look bowlegged and ski with their feet close together; their outside knee might wobble in and out during a hard turn. As with undercanting, overcanting is usually easy to see in a straight run. When turning, the skier might push the hip out in the turn's initiation to make the ski slip or de-angulate with the knee by pushing it to the outside, and might turn with too much weight on the inside ski because it has less of an edge than the outside ski.

Skiers obsessed with carving sometimes overcant their boots because it makes the ski rail so well without them having to do much themselves. The common negative side effects are an overly square stance with no hip angulation or counter, stiffness in the midbody, an overall robotic look, and difficulty with variable terrain and snow.

FIGURE 10.13   An overcanted skier in a turn.

It's common for people to need different amounts of cant in each boot. Even if your boots' canting is in the ballpark, each ski will behave differently if one boot is off by a degree or two. Your skis won't change edges at the same time turning to the left as turning to the right and, given the same amount of angulation, one ski will hold better and turn more sharply than the other.

Determining Proper Lateral Cant

Do you need to adjust your boots' cant? You won't know until you try. And even if the final answer is no, it's worth experimenting with cants because the experience teaches you some important lessons about how your edges work. You don't need special equipment—just some simple, common workshop tools, some firm snow to ski on, some simple materials you can find at any ski area, such as trail maps, and the willingness to experiment. Trail maps are a good size and thickness for shimming your ski boots in just the right places to jimmy the canting, and they're always available. Some of the best instructors I know swear by them. Good alternatives are sheets of rubber, plastic, or cork cut into 4-inch (10 cm) squares. A lot of boots have built-in gizmos intended for adjusting their lateral cant, but some are ineffective, and none are as convenient to work with as a simple trail map.

Start by making some basic measurements, which you can do with a boot fitter or by yourself using some simple tools and procedures we'll describe shortly. Many systems have been devised over the years to determine the right amount of lateral canting for a skier, and the better ones work well for many people. But none of them work for everyone, and there are some people for whom none of them work. Look at these systems as a good place to start. In some cases, that starting point will end up being just right, and in other cases it will just get you close.

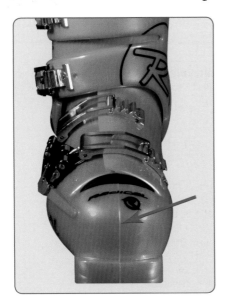

The most successful measurement systems are all based on a common idea: When viewing the skier in the frontal plane, a line perpendicular to the sole of the boot and passing through the geometric center of the knee should pass through the skier's foot somewhere in the vicinity of the crotch between the first and second toes, usually approximated by the mold line in the plastic at the toe of the boot's shell (figure 10.14). This works for most skiers, but isn't 100 percent reliable for everyone. Very precise and repeatable tool sets that work on this principle are available at ski shops, but you can get results that are just about as good with simple tools like a plumb bob and a carpenter's level or a carpenter's square. The procedure for using these tools is shown in figure 10.15. You can improve the precision of your results by repeating the procedure a few times and calculating the average of the measurements.

Once you've determined how much cant adjustment is needed, the boots are adjusted by shimming the cuffs, planning the soles, adjusting a mechanism built into the boot for the purpose, or some other method.

FIGURE 10.14 The boot's mold line.

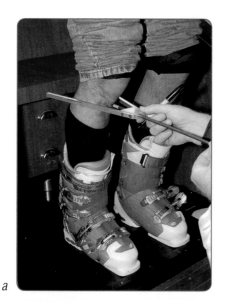

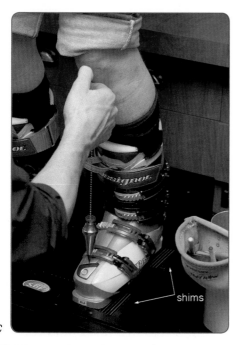

shims

a

b

c

d

FIGURE 10.15   Measuring lateral cant alignment: *(a)* Regardless of the particular tools used, start by buckling the boots tight and marking the knee's geometric center at the top of the tibia, just below the kneecap. Use a ruler to find the center if you don't have a special tool for this. *(b)* If you're using a plumb bob, establish a level platform, either with a plate that can be adjusted, as shown, or by using a carpenter's level to find a hard, level floor. *(c)* Hang the plumb bob from the mark on the knee, then place shims under one edge of the boot sole or the other until the plumb bob lines up with the boot's mold line. The tilt produced by the shims corresponds to the amount the boot's cant needs to be adjusted. *(d)* A carpenter's square can be used to get the same results as a plumb bob. You need a hard, flat surface to stand on, but it need not be perfectly level. Place the square so that its vertical leg is aligned with the boot's mold line. Then place shims under the boot, as in the plumb-bob method, until the mark on the knee is also aligned with the carpenter's square.

Equipment used in figures *a-c* courtesy of Ski Boot Fitting, Vail, Colorado.

FIGURE 10.16 Use trail maps to experiment with cant adjustments. Trail maps, the industry standard for this purpose among ski instructors, are durable, a perfect size and thickness, and readily available for on-hill experimentation.

There are different, essentially equivalent ways to shim the boots that work for whichever set of tools you use to make the measurements. If you're doing this yourself, the best way to shim is by putting trail maps or some material of similar size and thickness between the shell and liner of your boots (figure 10.16). This might require different adjustments for each boot. And if your boots already fit tightly around your ankles, you might need to adjust the placement of the buckle hardware for the top two buckles on your boots.

These methods provide a good starting point. It's not clear, however, how well they take into account several factors that might affect canting:

- How the alignment of the knee might change as the leg is flexed and extended at the knee and hip.

- The leg's Q angle—the angle between the lines of the femur and tibia when viewed in the frontal plane.

- Whether the skier's legs naturally rotate inward or outward (pigeon toed, duck footed, knock-kneed or bowlegged).

- Perhaps most important, the fact that when the skier is most concerned with controlling the edge—when in a turn—the large majority of weight is on the outside ski, the pelvis is tilted outward slightly relative to the balance axis, and the skier is countered at least a bit and is effectively standing on the edges of the boots rather than flat on the soles.

As I said, after making these measurements and boot adjustments, you'll now be at a good starting point. The next step is to do some on-snow testing to zero in on the right amount of cant. Go skiing on some hard, smooth snow, starting off with some pivot slips (see chapter 5). Make turns of various sizes and shapes at different speeds, and try some straight running, too. After skiing a couple of runs, add some more trail maps to each boot, and try again. Then take some trail maps out. Then move the trail maps to the other side of your boots, to change things radically in the other direction, and ski some more. Try different amounts of cant in each boot, too. Remember: Until you know how too much feels and how too little feels, you won't know what's right.

After a day of experimenting on firm to hard snow, you should have a good idea of what canting is all about, and an opinion of what works best for you. (If the snow is soft, you might not feel much difference.) Don't worry if you seem to like different degrees of canting on each boot. This is common. More durable materials than trail maps for experimenting are rubber, plastic, and cork. They can also be glued to the liner for more permanent adjustments if they don't change the fit of the cuff too much. If your boots have a built-in cant-adjustment mechanism, try using it, but don't be surprised if it seems to have little effect.

When you're sure how much lateral cant adjustment you want, go see your boot fitter for more permanent adjustments. He'll propose either making the cuff adjustments permanent in one way or another, or canting the whole boot by canting the soles. The most common way to cant soles is to plane them at an angle with specialized power tools, then screw plates to the toes and heels of the boots to restore them to their original thickness, ensure they work properly with your bindings, and add some tread so you can walk in them without slipping. You can also increase or reduce the boots' forward lean at this time by using plates of different thicknesses under each toe and heel. This is not a job to be undertaken by someone without a lot of experience.

One last note: If your boots are canted perfectly for you when they're brand new, they may be undercanted after 10 or 20 days of skiing, depending on the thickness of their liners: As they compress with use, the effective cant of the boots can decrease. So it's probably best to ski in a new pair of boots for a bit before you make permanent modifications to them.

Should you cant the cuff or the sole? This common question is hard to answer definitively. Both methods change the angle of the lower leg to the bottom of the boot, moving the knee laterally. The differences have to do with the difficulty of making the adjustment and how it affects the ankle. In addition to moving your knee laterally, canting the sole tilts the foot, yielding the same effect as described on page 163. Canting the cuff won't tilt the foot or move the ankle, but those effects can be achieved by tilting the footbed inside the boot as described earlier.

How much cant is optimal? The answer is different for every foot on every skier. There's little doubt that an accomplished skier can feel a 1-degree change in cant on hard snow. But it's not always clear what's optimal or that there even is an optimal cant for any one skier on all skis and in all snow conditions. Phil and Steve Mahre reportedly changed the canting in their boots from year to year. Some great skiers simply take their new boots out of the box and go skiing. Others tinker constantly.

Other Adjustments

The "big three" boot adjustments—custom footbeds, forward lean, and lateral canting—is all the tweaking many skiers need to get their boots adequately dialed in. You can reap further benefits, however, by attending to a few more subtle modifications.

Heel Lifts

Placing a heel lift inside the boot can help solve several boot problems. The main effect for many skiers, especially those who have limited range of motion in the ankle joint between the bottom of the tibia and the top of the talus, is to help match the axis about which the ankle flexes and the range of that flexion with the axis about which the boot wants to flex and the boot's range of flexion (figure 10.17). It's net effect is to make the front of the boot feel as if it better matches the travel of your leg when you bend your ankle. (You are, in fact, trying to make the movement of your leg match the flex of the boot.)

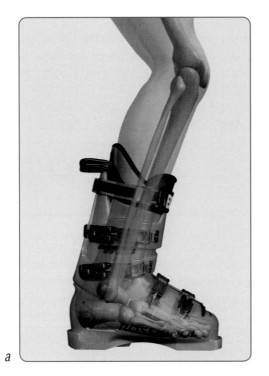 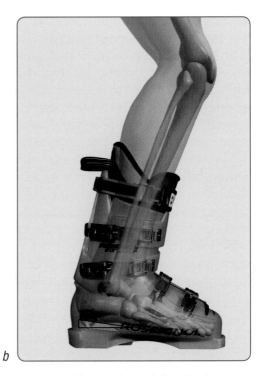

a   *b*

FIGURE 10.17   Putting a heel lift inside the boot, as shown in figure *b*, has several effects on the boot's fit and performance.

Raising your heel inside the boot will also make the boot fit tighter on the instep and change the alignment of the ankle bones (the *malleoli*) with the cups built into the liner and shell. This can be a good thing if you have a low instep, or if your malleoli don't line up well with the cups. If you need to raise your heel and it causes fitting problems, consult a good boot fitter.

Adding a heel lift inside the boot increases the *ramp angle*, which isn't the same thing as increasing the boot's forward lean. A heel lift moves your center of gravity forward a bit, but not by much. All other things being equal, placing a quarter-inch (.6 cm) heel lift in a boot with a 5-degree ramp angle (the angle between the bottom of your foot and a horizontal line in the sagittal plane). Note that this and 18 degrees of forward lean will move your center of gravity forward by about a tenth of an inch (.25 cm). By comparison, increasing the forward lean by 2 degrees, a small adjustment, in the same boot will move your center of gravity forward about a half-inch (1.2 cm)—five times more.

Radial Canting

Getting the outside ski's forebody to bite early in the turn is essential to making the ski carve as early as possible. Key to getting the forebody to bite is pressing into the cuff of the boot in the right spot. When viewing the boot from above, in the transverse plane, that spot is at about 10 to 11 o'clock for the right boot, and 1 to 2 o'clock for the left boot.

Phil and Steve Mahre have talked about controlling the response of the ski in this regard by what they call "radial canting," which involves turning the cuff in the transverse plane by adjusting the points at which it's riveted to the lower part of the shell. This is, of course, something that few of us can experiment with. But an easy way to produce a similar effect is by adding some shim material between the shell and liner in the 10 to 11 o'clock and 1 to 2 o'clock areas, as shown in figure 10.18. (This is another place where trail maps work well for on-hill experimentation.) As with lateral canting, don't be surprised if you find that you prefer different adjustments in your left and right boots.

Toe-Out

In recent years, several boot manufacturers have produced models that position the feet so they are toed slightly outward. The chief result of this is to change the alignment of the ankle's hinging axis, which has an effect something like that of radial canting: that is, it increases the carving response of the ski's forebody early in the turn.

At the elite competitive level, acceptance of this innovation has been varied. Some athletes like it, and some prefer a setup with no toe-out. Just as with lateral canting and forward lean, there's no reason to assume that everyone will ski their best if their boots are aligned the same in this respect. Unfortunately, there's no easy way to adjust toe-out for most boots. Perhaps some manufacturer will begin producing boots onto which sole plates with differing degrees of toe-out can be attached.

Customized Tongues

The fit of your boots over the bend in the front of your ankle, just behind the bony bump on your instep (formed by the intermediate cuneiform bone), is of paramount importance (figure 10.19). If the boot is at all loose there, you'll lose a lot of precision in your skiing. If it's too tight, it cannot only be painful but restrict blood flow to your toes.

One good way to tighten up the fit here is to build up the inside of the tongue in this area with thin pieces of adhesive-backed felt, such as Dr. Scholl's

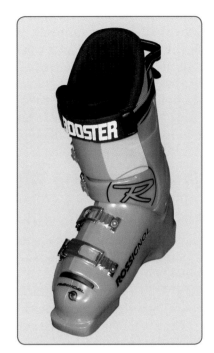

FIGURE 10.18 You can produce the effect of radial canting by putting a shim between the liner and cuff in the area indicated.

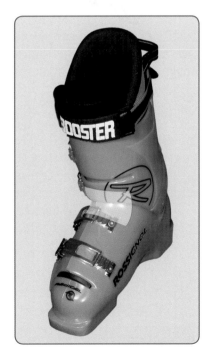

FIGURE 10.19 The fit of the boot in this area is critical. Customizing the fit of the tongues here, or replacing them with a custom foam pair, can significantly improve the fit and performance of your boots.

Moleskin. Be careful not to put too much pressure on the intermediate cuneiform, however. A better solution yet, and one that addresses too tight a fit in this area, is fitting your boots with foam-injected tongues, which are available from some suppliers of complete foam-injected ski boot liners, such as Conform'able. A pair of these custom foam tongues, when injected by an experienced boot fitter, can be the touch of perfection, making the boot fit so well over the instep that you get the same level of precision by buckling your boots comfortably that you used to get by clamping them down like vises.

Coming to Grips With Your Boots

The path to optimal fit and performance in ski boots lies somewhere between compulsive obsession and casual disregard, with the healthy recognition that perfection is not attainable and probably not even a meaningful concept when it comes to ski boots. On the other hand, if you put in the effort to get them dialed in, you should be able to get top performance out of your boots all day without having to unbuckle them, other than to warm them up on a cold day.

Once you think you've got a new pair set up just right, don't forget about them. Your feet change over the course of your life, the course of a season, and even the course of a day. Your boots change, too, especially the liners. So if your boots get more and more comfortable over time without you having done any work on them, take that as a sign that they've loosened up and their performance is quite possibly getting worse. Whenever someone says to me that they've had their boots so long that they feel like slippers, I figure those boots probably ski like slippers, too.

Don't take as gospel anyone's judgments but your own. Different skiers ski their best with different setups. Some of the best skiers in the world excel with setups that look overcanted. Others prefer less aggressive boots. A potential danger with any boot fitter or cant measurement system is that skiers who subscribe to them as sources of absolute truth transfer responsibility for their skiing ability to the measurement device and the boot fitter using it. Don't assume that your boots are perfect because someone else tells you so, no matter who it is. You have to feel the difference yourself. This is especially true if that person measures your stance indoors but doesn't watch you ski before and after adjusting your boots. No one's measurement system, regardless of how scientific or precise it might seem, is as relevant to your skiing as your own experience.

So take the time to toy with your boots now and then, even if you think they're spot-on. But don't drive yourself or your boot fitter crazy, either. At some point, it's time to just go skiing.

PART III

Matching Tactics and Technique to Real-World Skiing

As sports go, skiing is very technical. We analyze the forces, the movements, and the motions, and engage in deep discussions about how this or that aspect of technique works, often as if we've never skied anything but smooth, perfectly managed snow on runs with consistent pitches matched to the maneuvers we wish to perform. I like to call this "conservatory skiing": choosing the turns you want to make and the techniques you want to use, then finding a slope with the perfectly graded pitch and properly managed snow to suit them. This sort of skiing reminds me of the school figures that used to be part of competitive figure skating. Like golfers spending time at the driving range, conservatory skiing is a good thing for skiers to do, and I'll admit that I enjoy doing it from time to time.

But skiing would be pretty dull if that's all there was to it. Skiing comes alive when you let the mountain take the lead and you ski from moment to moment, making tactical decisions based on the natural snow conditions and terrain you find in front of you. What kind of turn would be the most fun to make against the side of that gulley? How fast do I want to go over that blind spot? Ultimately, the movements you make—the techniques you pull from your repertoire—are driven by these tactical decisions. This type of skiing is the polar opposite of conservatory skiing and is where the real fun and excitement lives. When the terrain and snow drive your tactics, and your tactics drive your technique, you're really skiing.

This final part of the book addresses four types of skiing conditions, each of which presents its own unique challenges and rewards: ice, moguls, powder, and steeps. Skiing each type well requires you to adopt particular tactics, including choice of equipment, and executing these tactics requires you to employ certain techniques. Each of these types of conditions deserves and receives its own chapter, focusing on the best tactics and techniques for handling it.

To call yourself an accomplished skier, you should be competent in all these situations. To be a true expert, you should be able to handle them with spirited self-assurance. The number of skiers who qualify as accomplished in each of these categories used to be much smaller than it is today. The great expansion of the ranks of good skiers is due almost entirely to advances in ski design. Before the appearance of shaped skis, the spectrum of those designs was one-dimensional. At one end, you had skis designed for beginners, and at the other, skis designed for racing. In between were racing skis that had been detuned by differing amounts to make them manageable by skiers of various skill levels. You picked a pair of skis based on how good a skier you were.

Things have changed. The spectrum is now two-dimensional. It still starts at one end with skis designed for beginners, but from there it fans out to take into account not only the ability of the skier but the terrain and snow for which the skis will be used. So now, instead of having essentially one type of ski for experts—racing skis—we also have all-mountain skis, backside skis, frontside skis, mogul skis, terrain park skis, and more. In fact, racing skis now occupy only a small niche in the high-performance ski market, and most expert skiers spend their time on other types of skis. These variations aren't just for a high-end market: They start to appear in skis intended for what ski schools consider advanced skiers—those who make parallel turns most of the time.

This broadening of the range of ski designs has had an interesting effect on how we ski: Good technique has become more unified and consistent across all terrain and snow conditions. Where we once thought differently about effective technique for moguls, powder, and hard snow, we now see skiers making more movements that are similar than movements that are different. To be sure, differences still remain, but there's no doubt that now, more than ever before, good technique is good technique, regardless of the slope and the snow, and improving in one setting will help your skiing in other settings. So if you don't really care for moguls, go work on your mogul skiing. It will help your powder skiing, and you'll probably get to like skiing moguls, too. Same thing with ice. Seek it out now and then, tune up your hard-snow skills, and your efforts will pay dividends on the steeps. Remember: The best skiers can rip on all terrain, in all snow. However focused your own aspirations are, you'll have a better chance of realizing them, and have more fun doing so, if you become a truly complete skier along the way.

Ice

FIGURE 11.1 Bode Miller nails two turns on his way to winning the giant slalom at Alta Badia, Italy. This venue is widely considered to have the most challenging giant slalom hill on the World Cup circuit. It's steep, it twists and turns relentlessly, and the snow is often extremely icy. Miller's skiing here is a textbook on attacking such conditions.

Ice is the most technically demanding surface we ski on. It's the calibrator. It measures our ability and spits back the judgment immediately. Small errors reap big consequences. Some things you can get away with on normal packed snow fail miserably on ice. But when you're skiing right, nobody else has to tell you, because the ice does. Holding an edge is, of course, the big issue, because without grip, speed and direction control go out the window, and things get sketchy fast. To hold a turn on hard ice requires the right tactics, equipment, and technique (figure 11.1). So the next time you watch an Olympic or World Cup ski race, and you see the best racers in the world attacking the course, carving lines that are aggressive at the bleeding edge of possibility, pause to consider that the surface under their skis is as hard as a hockey rink. What these athletes are doing is every bit as difficult and impressive as completing a long touchdown pass into heavy coverage, sinking a long putt on a fast, undulating green, or hitting a major league fastball.

Equipment

There's a reason why World Cup skis are narrow under the foot: It gives them optimal grip, as explained in the discussion in chapter 8 on edge control. If you're going to spend much time on boiler-plate surfaces, ditch the all-mountain midfats and ski on something that's 70 millimeters or narrower underfoot. And regardless of the skis you use, make sure you've got at least 10 millimeters of lift under the bindings.

Your skis must be sharp! Ski hard on a sharp ski for one day on ice, and that ski will no longer be sharp enough. (World Cup skiers today typically use 4- to 5-degree side bevels for slalom and 3-degree side bevels for giant slalom. These bevels require great skill to handle and get dull very quickly.) Your boots are just as critical as sharp skis. It's not as important that your boots be stiff as that they fit snugly with minimal play, and that they are canted properly (see Lateral Canting in chapter 10).

Tactics

If you find yourself on what looks to be challenging ice, start with some short sideslips to a stop to get a feel for things. Then make some conservative turns, staying in a flexed, centered, athletic stance. Keep your speed in check, and if the snow's super hard, accept the fact that you'll be making some controlled skids rather than clean, carved arcs.

Once you can manage your speed and direction well enough to feel that you're in control of the situation, it's time to consider how to attack real turns. Holding a turn on ice hinges on two simple principles: It's harder to make a ski hold a big steering angle than a small one, and, once a ski has started skidding, it's hard to get it to hook up again and start carving. The conclusion to be drawn from these principles is that you want to start the ski carving early in the turn if you can, when holding is relatively easy, and carve through to the completion, where holding is more difficult. Instead of just putting your skis sideways and then trying to make them grip, you want to get the skis engaged in the snow surface by the time they're in the fall line, or shortly thereafter, by getting them up on edge and applying pressure to them.

Look ahead and anticipate changes in the snow. If the snow surface is inconsistent, with patches of ice interspersed with hard snow, target the softer areas for the carving phase of your turns, and plan your transitions for the hardest spots. If you're in the middle of a turn and see a glassy patch of ice coming up, ease up on the turn a little and target the next softer area for shutting things back down. Don't forget that the snow is usually softer at the sides of the trails than in the middle.

FIGURE 11.2 Lasse Kjus of Norway, one of the best all-around skiers of all time, is a picture of stability and control on hard snow. He has just enough pressure on his inside ski to help him control the carving of his outside ski. His arms are even and held in a posture that clearly aids his balance.

Techniques

The ski that most needs to be on edge and have force applied to it is the outside ski. It's good to have a bit of weight on your inside ski for balance and stability, but when it comes to carving an arc on really hard snow and ice, the outside ski is the one that does the work (figure 11.2).

"Getting the ski on edge" means getting the ski both to a high edge angle and an aggressive platform angle of 90 degrees or less (see The Ski's Platform Angle in chapter 2). The high edge-to-snow angle is required so the ski can be bent into reverse camber, and the aggressive platform angle will make it hold. Edge-to-snow angle is determined primarily by body inclination, so to get the skis edged early, your upper body must be committed into the turn early. (But don't overdo it, either. If you overcommit, you'll either end up with too much weight on your inside ski or have to pivot your skis to prevent this from happening.) At the same time, use hip and knee angulation to control the ski's platform angle. In particular, early knee angulation is important for making the ski start to carve early in the turn.

Getting early pressure on the forebody of the outside ski in these turns is essential. It requires you to move your body forward as it goes across the feet in the transition. A good method for doing this is to think about moving your hips forward into the new turn. Do this by keeping your torso flexed forward from the waist and through the spine. Through the carving phase and into the turn's completion, move pressure progressively toward the middle of the ski by straightening your ankle. In some cases, you might end the turn with pressure focused at the rear of your foot's arch, and with some pressure on the back of the boot cuff. But in all cases, you must keep your torso flexed forward. Whether and how much you shift pressure back depends mostly on the radius and shape of the turn, and the length and sidecut of your skis: In general, the tighter the turn's radius and the longer the ski's length and sidecut radius, the farther forward you'll be throughout the turn (figure 11.3).

FIGURE 11.3 Ted Ligety moves forward going into these slalom turns, and finishes them on his heel. The best way to think about the forward movement is moving the hips forward; the best way to think about the aft movement is straightening the ankle or moving the outside foot forward. Note that the torso is forward at all times, and the fore–aft adjustments are made with the ankles.

Because the support of the edged ski in the snow is more tenuous than it is on softer snow, fore–aft balance and the distribution of pressure along the outside ski are more critical. Pressure too far forward, and the tail slips; too far back, and the ski shoots away to the outside of the turn, leaving you in the backseat on your inside ski. If you're going to err in one direction or the other, it's better to be too far forward than too far back.

As I said, if the tail of the outside ski slips, particularly in the last third of the turn, you're too far forward. The fix is, once again, to straighten your ankle to bring the foot forward a bit. But at the same time you have to maintain knee angulation. This skill—sliding the outside foot forward and backward while independently controlling the edge with knee angulation—is a subtle one that's worth working on. A good exercise to develop this movement, described in chapter 5, is moving your feet forward and back while turning in a tuck. Add to this movement the focus of maintaining strong knee angulation as you straighten your ankles and move your feet forward in the last third of the turn (figure 11.4).

FIGURE 11.4 Markus Larsson's skiing makes the ice look soft with a quiet upper body and active legs and feet. His torso and arms are relaxed, yet barely move except to clear the gates and make pole plants, and his hips are quiet and controlled as they move diagonally through the transition. Beneath this stable mass, his feet and legs control the edges and fore–aft pressure on the skis. Notice how he maintains his knee angulation while flexing and straightening his ankles.

The most common error skiers make on ice is to extend and stiffen the downhill leg when things get dicey. This is usually accompanied by the hip going out over the downhill ski and the upper body tipping uphill. These are instinctive, psychologically driven actions that hinder rather than help. When your downhill leg is straight and stiff, it's virtually impossible to angulate at the knee or the hip. Pushing the hip out flattens the skis, increasing their platform angle and making them slide. Tipping the body uphill reduces the force on the downhill ski just when you need as much force as you can get to drive the edge into the snow surface. If you find yourself tipping into the hill, flex your entire body to a lower, more athletic posture, turn your upper body to face the direction your skis are sliding, and grit it out. Get your weight on your downhill ski, and use knee and hip angulation to maintain an aggressive platform angle.

CHAPTER 12

Moguls

Moguls add wonderful variety to skiing. Like running race courses and skiing in trees, moguls demand that you turn where and when they want you to turn. In doing so, they focus your attention like few things I know of, and when you're moving in synch with them, locked into the line, you feel coupled with the snow in a way that's hard to verbalize but that every good mogul skier understands and appreciates. To reach that point, you need to be familiar with the nature of the moguls (figure 12.1 provides some of the terminology we'll use), how to formulate the best line through them, and the key technical movements you need to make to ski that line.

Equipment

Grip and carving on an edge are seldom an issue in moguls, so stiff boots and edgy, deeply shaped skis aren't necessary. Although general-purpose ski equipment is fine in moguls for most people, competitive mogul skiers favor softer flexing boots (something you can simulate by loosening your top buckle) and relatively narrow skis with traditional sidecuts. And because they must make precise pole plants on every turn in a deeply flexed position, competitive mogul skiers use shorter poles than we use for general skiing.

Tactics

Every field of moguls is a puzzle to be solved. And like any nontrivial puzzle, you have a better chance of solving it if you have a tool kit of proven strategies and tactics with which to attack it. Regardless of how well you've honed your technique, if you can't find a good, workable line through a field of bumps, you're in for a rough ride.

The best strategy for a field of challenging bumps is to find a comfortably smooth path through the field at a manageable speed. Where you make your turns, how you shape them, and where you act to control your speed—these are the tactical moves you make to solve the puzzle. The best way I know of to find the line and the speed control points in moguls involves a two-step process for each turn. Each step is based on an essential fact about moguls.

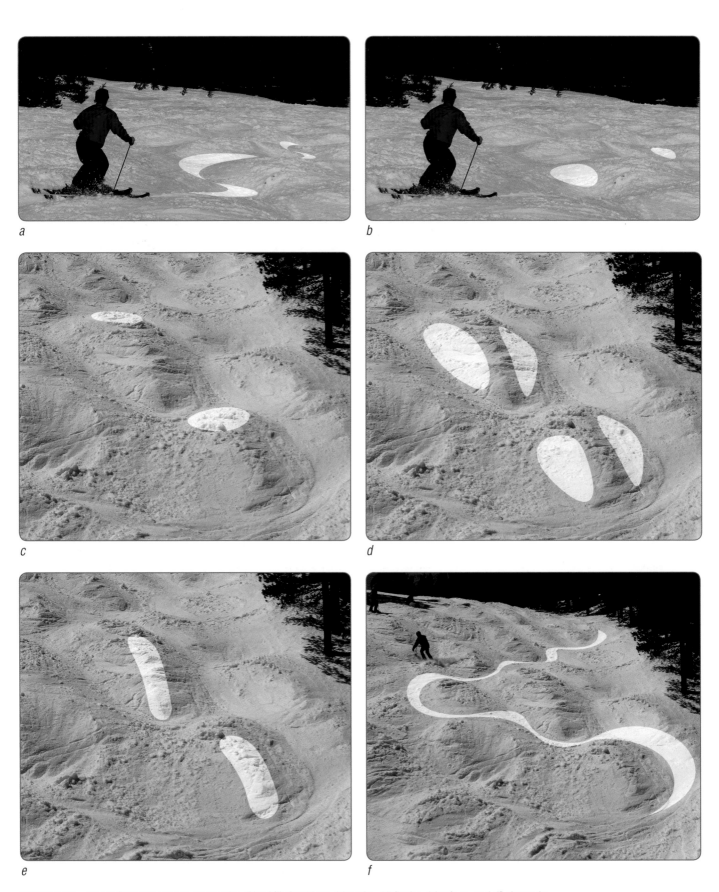

FIGURE 12.1 Mogul field geography: *(a)* troughs, *(b)* uphill shoulders, *(c)* peaks, *(d)* flanks, *(e)* spines, and *(f)* channels.

Fact 1: There's only one reliably good place on a mogul to check your speed: the uphill shoulder (figure 12.1). Here is where the snow is softest and where snow that slides down from the bump above collects. This soft snow, as well as the flatness of this part of the mogul, makes it easy to set your edges here. Finally, there's less likely to be a nearby mogul in a position to catch your tails.

Fact 2: The smoothest line through a field of moguls—the one that best avoids those parts of the mogul that most threaten your stability—generally follows the troughs (figure 12.1*a*) from start to finish and passes through those very spots that are your best control points: the bumps' uphill shoulders.

FIGURE 12.2   Spotting the control points. In this challenging mogul field, the skier is constantly looking down the hill, searching for good control points on the uphill shoulders of moguls. She knows where she'll end each turn well before she starts it. This particular slope, Mach 1 at Breckenridge, Colorado, has been the site of many World Cup mogul competitions, and is well known for its steep pitch and deep moguls. The camera doesn't do it justice. Skier: Jenn Metz.

Now that we have the two essential facts, here is our two-step process for finding our line.

Step 1: Pick your control point. Before you start the turn, decide where you're going to finish it. Look down the hill to find a good uphill shoulder where you'll be able to shed some speed if you need to. This spot will usually be one of the moguls just below the one you're on (figure 12.2).

Step 2: Find the smoothest line that will take you from where you are to the control point you picked in step 1. In most cases this will follow the trough between the mogul you're on and the next one over. In some cases, you might want to bank against the bump on the far side of the trough, or carve down the flank (figure 12.1*d*) of the bump you're turning around. Your choice depends on the contour of the snow and the speed you want to go. But, in all cases, you want your skis to be pointed at all times in the direction the trough runs. If you try to put them sideways, your tails stand a good chance of catching on the bump at the far side of the trough.

You've got to accept that you'll pick up some speed in the trough. But if you know where your upcoming control point is, you don't have to worry about that. Instead, you can focus on fitting your skis into the shape of the trough so that you get a smooth ride to the end of the turn (figure 12.3). Most skiers are afraid of picking

FIGURE 12.3   The smoothest line from one control point to the next follows the trough from its very beginning, out and around the mogul, not sliding down its flank. Skier: Cait Boyd.

up speed in bumps, so they try to keep their speed in check throughout the turn. They often ski into the flank of the mogul, then pivot their skis when they reach the peak or the spine (figure 12.1, *c* and *e*, p. 186), because it's easy to swivel them there. That leaves the skiers with their skis sideways on the steep, often icy, flank on the other side of the mogul. From here, they slide sideways down that flank and bang into the bottom of the trough, where the skis' sideways motion exposes them to catching their tails or an outside edge.

Contrast this with seasoned bump skiers who, at the start of the turn, let their skis run straight across the bump's uphill shoulder into the very beginning of the trough on the far side of the bump, and then turn them only enough to conform to the line of the trough. Turning them farther will cause the tails to catch. These skiers might pick up some speed through the turn, but this is the smoothest, most stable line, and they know they'll be able to slow down when they reach the control point.

Making one turn around one mogul is, of course, just a start. You have to constantly look ahead for the next control point and, if you're good, you'll be looking farther ahead than that a lot of the time. Riveting your eyes to the mogul right in front of you is like looking at the hood of your car in highway traffic. You want to get into a rhythm with your eyes: When you're in the middle of the trough, look down the hill to pick a control point for the end of the next turn. Once you've got it, turn your eyes back to the control point of the turn you're in. As you ski up to it, scan the trough on the far side of the shoulder for the line through the next turn. Occasionally, look farther down the hill to get an advanced view of the future. Repeat.

Once you understand the basics of line finding, you'll want to develop a repertoire of tactical tools to deal with the endless variety of situations you'll find in moguls. Here are a just few.

Moguls on a Sidehill.   It's often hard to find good, long, continuous lines through moguls on a sidehill. On a slope that falls away to the left, for instance, you can usually find good lines for your turns to the right, but often your turns to the left will take you into a wall. One tactic that works in these situations is to ski near one edge of the slope or the other. The lines there will be simpler. The moguls on the uphill side of the slope will also be smaller. The moguls on runs with sidehills will often form up in rows across the hill, and a workable tactic for these places is to look for lines that go across the hill between rows. You can make several turns in a row through one of these channels while keeping your eyes out for a good place to make a turn or two back across the grain of the mogul field (figure 12.1*f*).

The Zipper Line.   The zipper line is the full-on fall-line assault on a mogul field that you see prosecuted by World Cup mogul skiers and other hot shots of the bumps. With the proper approach and the right field of moguls, you can learn to ski this line yourself (probably in tamer moguls).

First, you've got to find the right mogul field. Look for one on a consistent, easy pitch with a dead-straight fall line. You want to start from a spot about five or six moguls from the bottom of the field, so if you start to lose it you'll have some smooth terrain to escape onto. Traverse slowly across the hill, looking carefully downhill for a rhythmic, symmetric pattern of bumps and troughs running to the bottom. That's your line. It's the sort of line that's deliberately manufactured for World Cup mogul courses and which allows the fastest fall-line bump skiing.

Your first time down, make round turns to keep your speed down. Ski the same line the same way until you feel completely comfortable with it. Then try skiing it a little bit straighter, not going completely out into the trough and around the bump in every turn, but more down the hill and over the bump. Finally, try skiing it straighter still, up to the point that you no longer feel comfortable. When you know how fast you can comfortably go and you can maintain your speed at that level, start your runs farther up the mogul field.

Short Turns Down the Spine. If the troughs in a section of moguls simply run too fast for you, it's often possible to find an occasional big mogul with a long spine down which you can make a few quick, short check turns. By staying up on the spine, keeping your tips and tails out of the trough, it's easy to pivot your skis. The snow is relatively soft on the spine, too, making it easy to set your edges.

Techniques

To ski moguls well, not only must your line conform to the shape of the snow, but so must your body. Think about driving a car on an old dirt road full of potholes and big rocks. The car's suspension works in consort with the road so you don't get bounced and jarred while you direct the car on a line that skirts the big bumps and dips. When you ski, your body provides its own suspension system, but one that's better than a car's in an important way: You can consciously and actively move your body in anticipation of those bumps and dips. Therein lies one of the keys to expert mogul skiing: being proactive rather than reactive.

Moving Up and Down

To conform to the terrain, you must flex and extend your entire body through a long range of motion to carefully control the amount of force the snow exerts on you. You flex deeply to prevent your center of gravity from being tossed upward by the moguls, and you extend to keep your skis in contact with the snow in the troughs. And you have to do this without your balance being disturbed in any way. This means going from a very tall stance to a very short one and back again in perfect synch with the terrain, over and over, without your balance moving fore and aft or side to side. Any motion of your center of gravity must be strictly straight up and down, where "up and down" means directly along the balance axis. This is the most crucial technical element to mogul skiing. You can get a start on developing this skill by doing the exercises in chapter 6.

It's obvious to most skiers that they need to flex to absorb the bump as they ski into it, but it's not so obvious that they also need to extend as they ski into the trough. This accounts for a common technical error: staying in a low stance through the entire turn. Stand up tall in the middle of the turn so you'll have maximum range to absorb the bump at the end of the turn if necessary (figure 12.4). Standing tall in the trough has other benefits, too. You get a better view of the terrain below to help you plan your line, and your muscles get a moment to relax.

FIGURE 12.4 Flexing and extending accurately through a long range without disturbing your balance is the single most important technical skill in mogul skiing. Don't forget to extend in the middle of the turn. If you don't, you won't be able to absorb much at the end. Other good examples are figures 5.2 (p. 78), 6.2 (p. 89), and 6.15 (p. 98). Skier: Andy Gould.

Controlling the Edge

Because good mogul skiing is largely a matter of fitting your skis to the shape of the snow in front of you, you have to make instantaneous line adjustments, both from turn to turn and within each turn. Often, you won't be able to get a good look at the whole trough until you're down in it, when a large clump of loose snow or a rock might appear in your line. These sorts of little surprises pop up all the time, and the skilled mogul skier is the one who can quickly adjust the line to deal with them.

These tactical adjustments require quick and precise edge-control movements. You tighten the line by edging the skis more; you loosen the line by flattening them and feathering their edges. As with movements along the vertical axis, these constant edge adjustments must be done without your balance changing in any way. Small adjustments can be made by modulating the knee angulation of both legs simultaneously. Bigger adjustments might require angulating or deangulating with the hips, pushing them out to flatten the skis, or dropping them into the turn to raise the edge angle.

Edgeset and Pole Plant

As I've said already, the end of the turn is your primary speed control point in moguls. You pick that spot before you start the turn, and then ski a line that takes you there. If you pick up speed along the way, you might have to deal with some significant force when you get there. To be effective with your edges at the control point, you must angulate accurately, especially at the hips. If you need to dump a lot of speed and must avoid catching an outside edge when you do, drop low and employ more hip angulation. To improve your lateral stability at the control point, you must plant your pole at the end of the turn, not at the beginning of the next one. Get the pole ready early. Good mogul skiers have their pole ready to plant when they're halfway through the turn. And when you plant it, plant it in the right place: Extend your arm well away from your body, and put the tip of the pole in the snow ahead of your hand (figures 12.4, p. 191, and 12.5).

FIGURE 12.5   Angulation and a solid, precise pole plant are essential in moguls. Get the pole ready to plant well before you need it. Skier: Jerry Berg.

CHAPTER 13

Powder, Crud, and Slush

Powder, crud, and slush are what I like to call loose snow—snow you ski *in* rather than *on*. This is, generally speaking, snow that has never been completely skied out and packed, the exception being spring snow that has softened so much that your skis sink into it as if it were unpacked. In these days of industrialized skiing on snow that's managed by large grooming machines resembling farming equipment, loose, unmanaged snow is an opportunity to be relished. You meet the mountain on its own terms, not those of the ski area's marketing department. The snow can change from turn to turn, and its variety and natural character engages you in a way that makes you feel closer to the alpine world around you (figure 13.1).

FIGURE 13.1　Skiing in untracked powder is one of the best experiences many of us will ever have. With modern equipment, good tactics, and the technique to bring them together, skiing in powder, crud, and slush can be enjoyed by any good skier. Skier: Derek Frechette.

Equipment

Skis that are relatively wide underfoot (80 mm or more) and longitudinally soft make skiing in unpacked snow easier, although all modern skis are far better in these conditions than anything available 15 years ago, other than powder-specific skis.

You certainly don't need stiff boots for these conditions, but they're not a liability, either. If you feel your boots are too reactive for the situation, simply leave the top buckle loose and control the forward flex by how tightly you cinch the power strap against the boot's tongue.

One piece of equipment I do think is worthwhile, especially in powder, is a pair of poles with full-size powder baskets. There are times when you want all the support you can get from your pole: torque from a blocking pole plant, lateral support for when you commit down the hill in a sketchy situation, something to push against so you can lift the skis out of the snow to start a turn in a tight spot, or simply something to help you climb out of a gully or pole across a flat. Those sexy little racing-style baskets that most high-end poles come with can be hopelessly inadequate here.

Tactics

As mentioned, you ski *on* packed snow, and you ski *in* powder, crud, and slush. Therein lies the key to understanding how to ski unpacked snow. Because your skis are *in* the snow, they can't move sideways easily. They're hard to pivot and hard to displace to the outside at the start of the turn. You can't make really short turns unless you apply a lot of torque to your skis or can get them up and out of the snow. This is reasonable in some situations, but in general it's better to adopt the tactic of making somewhat larger turns than you would make on the same slope if the snow were packed. In particular, you can't rush the top half of the turn. You must give it more time to develop than you might on a packed slope, and accept the fact that, in order to make turns, you'll need to go faster and have more momentum than you would on packed snow.

FIGURE 13.2 Kicking your tails in the snow makes it easier to start off straight down the hill, so your first turn is only a half-turn out of the fall line. This is much easier than trying to start your first turn from a traverse. Skier: Bob Rankin.

Let yourself pick up some speed before making your first turn. Pointing your skis straight down the hill when you take off will help get you up to speed, and it will make your first turn just a half-turn and much easier to execute (figure 13.2). Avoid starting from a traverse if you can. But if you must, start your first turn with an uphill stem. Once you start turning, keep turning—make the end of one turn be the start of the next. Pick a rhythm and stick with it. Whatever you do, don't go into a traverse at the end of a turn. Starting a turn from a traverse is much harder than making a turn that's linked with the one before.

An important tactical decision you need to make concerns finding the best snow to ski in. Untracked powder that hasn't been hit by wind is the best of all loose snow conditions because of its consistency. Cut-up powder, crud, and slush are progressively more difficult because your skis can slow down and speed up erratically, and clumps of snow can knock your tips around or grab an outside edge. The toughest to ski is loose snow that has developed a substantial but breakable crust; this snow will catch the outside edges of all but the best skiers.

Exposure to sun and wind is the biggest factor affecting the quality of loose snow. You can count on the lightest, fluffiest snow being on north-facing slopes, in the shade. If the snow has been hit by wind, seek out downwind exposures. If you're having trouble finding snow that hasn't been drifted, ski near the trees on the upwind side of the slope. Exposure is particularly important when hunting for good slush in the spring. Like a good peach, if you don't let it get enough sun and warmth before you try it, it will be too hard to enjoy. If, on the other hand, you wait too long, it will be too wet and sloppy. The key to finding good slush is to track the optimal exposure as the day goes on: Start by skiing eastern-facing pitches; then migrate around through more southerly exposures, and finish up facing west.

Several tactics can help you find the least-tracked snow, and also help you deal with the tracks that you can't avoid. First of all, the terrain you can see from the lift is always going to be skied up more than any place else, so think about looking elsewhere. Look for islands of trees and places where the slope suddenly widens. Because skiers tend to go more or less straight down the fall line, tree islands cast a sort of "skier shadow," and the snow just below them doesn't get skied much. Cut in tight under them, and you're likely to find powder when the rest of the slope is tracked out. If the trail is north facing, the snow below an island will also be shaded from the sun, and thus drier and lighter than the snow out in the middle of the run. Where the snow has been tracked, you'll find you'll get much better turns by skiing a line at an angle to everyone else's general direction of travel. This works particularly well on runs with a counterslope, where everyone tends to follow the general direction of the run. Get on the uphill side of the run, then make turns down the true fall line to the other side of the slope. Once you get there, turn hard and traverse back to the high side of the run and do it again. You can get surprisingly good turns this way.

I have one more important thing to say about finding good loose snow: Never ski under the ropes into closed areas. It's not cool; it's foolish. Ski areas close off sections of the mountain for good reasons, almost always related to your safety. The mountain managers and ski patrol know better than anyone, including you, where it's safe to ski and where it isn't.

Techniques

Every parallel turn on skis begins with establishing an inclined relation between your center of gravity and your feet. This can be accomplished by the feet moving to the outside of the new turn or the center of gravity moving to the inside, or a combination of the two. Whether they realize it or not, most skiers start most of their turns by sliding their skis sideways to the outside. Once the skis have gotten sideways enough and edged enough to build up some pressure, they make the skier's path start to bend.

This approach works adequately on packed snow, but it doesn't fare as well in loose snow because the skis can't move sideways very easily. To get them to do so, inexperienced powder- and junk-snow skiers heave their bodies upward to free their skis from the snow and hurl themselves around to put enough torque and force

FIGURE 13.3 An uphill stem is a good technique for getting the new outside ski up on its edge and establishing inclination in a tight spot at slow speeds. Skier: Carol Levine.

FIGURE 13.4 Hip rotation is useful for powering a turn when the terrain is moderate or when you need extra power to start a turn in heavy snow. However, you need to stop the rotation and pull your hips back toward the inside of the arc to make your skis shape the lower half of the turn. Skier: Derek Frechette.

on their skis to plow them sideways toward the outside of the new turn. This is an exhausting and inefficient way to ski. It's also inherently unstable because moving the skis sideways through the snow makes you prone to catching an outside edge.

The best way to establish the required inclination is by letting your center of gravity move to the inside of the new turn, rather than making the skis move to the outside. Chapter 9, Lateral Balance, discussed good techniques for this. That's the ideal, anyway, and it works when the hill has enough pitch, when you've got enough momentum and enough room to make the turn, and when you've committed your body perfectly going through the transition. In practice, many turns in these conditions require at least a bit of rotation, either from the hip or shoulders, to help power the turn. These techniques are described in chapter 7.

There are plenty of times when even a bit of rotation doesn't get the job done—you're going too slowly, the snow's too heavy, or you've got to pull off a clutch turn in the trees—so you have to haul out the heavy artillery and toss off full rotations with your hips and upper body. It's worth practicing these techniques so you've got them when you need them (figure 7.16, p. 116). Another option, good for tight places at low speeds or when you need to start your first turn from a traverse, is a simple uphill stem (figure 13.3).

When the pitch is flat to moderate and the snow is more than a few inches (5+ cm) deep, rhythm, bounce, and up-unweighting will help a lot. Hip rotation, combined with up-unweighting, might be your primary tool to get your skis turning and pushed to the outside of the turn (figure 13.4). But as the hill gets steeper and your speed increases, leg rotation should be your primary mechanism for turning the skis (figure 13.5), and hip rotation should become more of a secondary technique to provide that extra little oomph you need to get the job done. If and when you do rotate with your hips, don't let your shoulders tip into the turn. Maintain their alignment in the frontal plane. The movement of your hips and torso should be, as much as possible, a pure rotation in the transverse plane.

Regardless of the situation, you should use only as much rotation as you need to get the turn started, and not continue to rotate through the control phase of the turn. When it's time to make the skis bend and shape the arc, you need to get your hips back in line with, or to the inside of, the balance axis.

The less firm the snow's base, the more weight you can put on your inside ski. In truly bottomless powder, 50-50 is the way to go. If you prefer a wide stance on packed snow, narrowing your stance in loose snow reduces the chances of crossing your tips. If you're skiing in a few inches of powder, say 6 inches (15 cm) or less on top of a packed base, you can use a hip-width stance and put most of your weight on the outside ski—the same stance and weight distribution you use on packed snow.

Keep your shoulders forward and your fore–aft balance around the middle of your feet (figure 13.6). Roll forward to the balls of your feet going into the turn and, as you approach the bottom of the turn, move your feet forward a bit in anticipation of your skis slowing down as they go deeper into the snow.

FIGURE 13.5 When you have sufficient speed and momentum, leg rotation is the technique of choice for turning. Skier: Bob Rankin.

FIGURE 13.6 Fore–aft balance in powder is not much different than on packed snow. Here the skier rolls forward into the turn, then moves slightly back going into the last third in anticipation of her skis sinking farther into the snow and slowing down. Skier: Dee Byrne.

Don't sit back! The claim that you have to sit back in powder, crud, and slush is one of the biggest myths in ski technique. Skiers inexperienced in these conditions are uncomfortable when they can't see their skis, and fear they'll dive into the snow and suddenly stop. But unless you're way too far forward, the skis' reverse camber and upturned tips prevent this from happening.

Slush is special. I love it, and so do most good skiers I know. The ability to ski slush is, to my mind, the measure of a skier's technique in loose snow. Slush presents the skis with more resistance to moving sideways than any other loose snow conditions, while providing the most support for carving when they're edged properly. Making turns in thick slush by shoving your skis around is tiring and difficult, and outside edges are easy to catch. That's why people who don't know how to ski slush don't like it. Making turns the right way, by letting your body fall diagonally across your skis into the new turn, then balancing against the skis as they carve through to the end of the turn against the firm support of that wet sloppy snow, is one of the great sensations of skiing (figure 13.7).

FIGURE 13.7   When deep slush hits its moment of perfect ripeness, it pegs the fun meter for a lot of good skiers. The keys to skiing in slush, as well as powder and crud, are for your body to move across your skis to get the turn started and to keep your skis moving forward, not sideways. Skier: Jenn Metz.

When unpacked snow develops a crust or inconsistent top layer, things become more difficult. It's best to avoid any attempt to move the skis laterally through such snow because the chance of catching an outside edge is high. In these situations, it's a good idea to get your skis up out of the snow in the transition, and to make sure they're up on their new edges before you come back down on them (figure 13.8). Otherwise, you're asking for trouble.

FIGURE 13.8   When loose snow has been hit by wind and gone through warm-to-cold cycles, it becomes inconsistent and sometimes develops a skin or crust. To deal with these challenging conditions, get your edges out of the snow in the transition, and don't come back down on them until your skis are tilted up on their new edges. Skier: Dan Egan.

The important techniques for skiing all types of loose snow are essentially the same. But certain conditions place a higher premium on certain techniques. As crud gets more cut up, powder gets more wind blown, or slush gets stickier and goopier, it becomes more important to pay attention to the fundamentals. Manage your fore–aft balance carefully, with your feet under a flexed, athletic stance and your hands up and in front of you. Move your body diagonally across your feet through the transition rather than trying to move the skis sideways through the snow. And use your legs independently, adjusting your weight between them as the situation calls for. Experts will tell you that good technique is basically good technique, and that when the snow is easy you simply get away with more mistakes.

Steeps

FIGURE 14.1 Steep? You bet. Fun? Yes, if you've got the chops.

For a skier, "steep" isn't about how many degrees a slope is pitched. It's about skill, experience, and temperament. "Steep" means a pitch that gets your attention and says, "You'd better ski well or there will be consequences." It means you've got to unhook your body from your emotions and take conscious, deliberate control of your actions. Just how many degrees it takes for a hill to be "steep" varies from skier to skier. A 35-degree pitch curls the toes of most competent recreational skiers; 40 to 45 degrees is a range that most experts find exciting. Steeper than that, and you'd better know what you're doing (figure 14.1).

Of course, it's easy to say "unhook your body from your emotions"; doing it is the tricky part. The best way to do it is to know the techniques that work best on steep terrain, then focus on execution when the situation calls for them. This chapter can help you with that knowledge. It's up to you to use it when your emotions threaten to take over.

Equipment

The best equipment for skiing steeps is dictated more by the snow conditions than anything else. If the snow is very hard, you want equipment similar to what you want for skiing ice (chapter 11). For steep, open terrain with loose or variable snow, wider, less edgy gear is better. Poles with full-size powder baskets come in handy for getting maximum torque and lateral support from your pole plant, as is often the case when you need to get your skis around quickly.

Tactics

Because falling on steep terrain is risky, the first order of business is stability. There are six keys to stability: keeping tight control on your speed; maintaining a flexed, athletic stance at all times; being conservative with your movements; keeping your fore–aft balance over your feet at all times; and last, but definitely not least, focusing the majority of your weight on the outside, or downhill, ski. This last key does two important things: First, it gives you the stability and edge you need to get good purchase with the snow. Second, it overcomes the deadly sin of steep skiing: the emotionally driven act of leaning into the hill, which leads to more catastrophes than any other error.

Most turns can be partially carved, but unless you've got a lot of room to work with and like going really fast, the initial steering angles will be big and the carving phases relatively short. In some cases the carving phase will all but disappear, and the best plan of attack for each turn is just to get your skis sideways quickly and plant them in the snow.

Because it's easy to pick up speed with every turn, speed control follows closely behind stability in importance. The first rule of speed control is to complete every turn well out of the fall line, so whatever excess speed you pick up in the first half of the turn is dissipated before you start the next one. Start off with short turns, and don't open them up until you know you've got things under control and feel comfortable with going faster. The second rule is to stay low and close to the snow. When the slope drops away steeply, it will do most of your unweighting for you. Any big extension and unweighting at the start of the turn will leave you flying at warp speed by the time you can exercise any control.

It's often a good idea to feel things out before you take the plunge on a slope you're unfamiliar with. Start by sideslipping a few feet and then sinking to a firm, decisive edgeset with a solid pole plant. Next (or start with this if you're in snow you can't sideslip through), jump down the hill sideways a foot or two, landing in that edgeset and pole plant, as shown in figure 14.2.

If you just don't feel confident about the situation because the snow is too funky, the hill drops away and you can't see what's on the other side, the pitch is too narrow or steep, or you've simply got the heebie-jeebies, let discretion be the better part of valor: Sidestep or sideslip down the hill to a place you feel comfortable.

FIGURE 14.2 Making a couple of sideways jumps helps you feel out the snow, settles you into a good position, and gets your spunk up. Skier: David N. Oliver.

The character of the snow can make a particular pitch fun or terrifying. If the snow you're standing on is iffy, don't hesitate to traverse to a more promising spot. The steep stuff is never groomed, and the feel of the snow can vary dramatically within a short space (figure 14.3).

FIGURE 14.3 Is the snow better on the right side or the left? Depending on a lot of factors—the time of year, the time of day, how warm it was yesterday, how long since it's snowed, and so on—one side could make you grin, and the other grit your teeth. This is the chute in the middle of the face in figure 14.1 (p. 200), seen from the top.

Techniques

For these tactics and techniques to work, you have to move forward on your skis going into the turn and be committed to the outside ski throughout. As long as you have enough speed and you're moving forward into the turn, leg rotation, a blocking pole plant, and some anticipation will supply all the torque you need to turn the skis. All this and more is shown in figure 14.4. If you're back on your heels, you'll need the extra oomph of some hip rotation. Because hip rotation involves moving so much of your mass around, your stability will likely be jeopardized, so use it sparingly. Picking up speed with each turn is usually the result of your balance being too

FIGURE 14.4   This pitch is 40 degrees. It might not look steep on the page, but trust me, it is. The skier moves forward into the turn, focuses on the downhill ski, plants her pole, and completes the turn with authority. Textbook technique makes the steep slope fun. Skier: Jenn Metz.

far back going into the turn or not completing the turn with your skis sufficiently across the fall line, or both.

As you do in moguls, focus on planting your pole at the end of the turn. If you think of planting it at the beginning of the next turn, it will come too late to provide the torque and lateral support you need in the transition. And get your pole ready to plant when you're in the fall line, well before you need it. If you wait until you're at the end of the turn to reach out to plant, you'll be late.

A classic technique for turning on very steep terrain is pedaling, shown in figure 14.5. Start by planting your pole solidly at an angle for maximum support laterally, vertically, and rotationally. Now, initiate the turn by extending upward from your uphill ski as you simultaneously pull your downhill ski up off the snow and swing its tip down the hill. The idea is to get the skis all the way around without spending any time in the fall line or using much space side to side. You're making a rotation turn, but most of the torque is coming from swinging the inside ski around, rather than your upper body. This gives you a lot of torque without throwing your hips and torso around. Once you can make linked ultrashort turns like this, try landing a little earlier and carving to the finish.

FIGURE 14.5 Pedaling. A big lift off the uphill foot and a swing of the downhill ski into the turn, supported with a solid blocking pole plant, powers a short turn that gets 'em around quickly on a steep slope without excessive upper-body movement. Skier: David N. Oliver.

It's not unusual on steep, smooth terrain to find yourself carving more than you really want and having trouble killing speed. If the snow conditions are amenable, you can scrub speed throughout the bottom half of the turn by pushing your hips to the outside of the turn a bit to flatten the skis, making them oversteer and slip. As you get to the end of the turn, bring your hip back to the inside of the turn to increase the ski's grip on the snow.

The biggest problem you'll often have on steep terrain is keeping your emotions from controlling your skiing. Apprehension puts you on your heels and on your uphill ski, and stiffens and straightens your body with clenched muscles. But overcoming your emotions doesn't mean eliminating them. It means accepting them but not letting them dictate your movements. Put them in the passenger seat and grab the wheel with forthright, deliberate, and effective movements— you'll experience the special exhilaration of overcoming fear with action.

Conclusion

We've gone through a lot of detail in this book—too much, certainly, to think about when you're out there on the hill making turns. So let me boil it down to a handful of simple guidelines:

- Tune in to the force from the snow, and judge what you're doing by how it feels. Feel for where your point of balance is and how your skis feel against the snow.
- Ski with your feet and balance with your body. Your feet and legs should be active; your upper body should be quiet.
- Focus on function, not form. Once you've got the first, the second will follow.
- Be multidimensional. Do drills and exercises to develop technical consistency and precision. Challenge yourself with terrain and snow to develop spontaneity and looseness.
- When you look for better skiers to emulate, pick the ones with simple styles. Avoid adopting flourishes, especially with the arms and hands, no matter who does them and how cool they look.

When others give you advice about your skiing, consider the following:

- Listen with an open mind. Half of the time you might think they're wrong, and half of those times you might be right. That means that the majority of the time, you'll learn something valuable.
- If a coach, instructor, or anyone else tells you something that doesn't make sense, don't nod your head as if it does. Ask for another explanation. Get into a dialog about it. But if the person still doesn't make sense, know when and how to politely move on.
- No one other than you can make you a better skier. The best coaches, instructors, and equipment technicians can help, but ultimately, it's up to you.

These words could have been written 30 years ago and been just as true then as they are today. There are other lasting truths about skiing: We ski in places that are beautiful and that many of us would otherwise seldom, if ever, visit. People can learn to ski before they can ride a bike and keep on skiing after they're too old to ride one. Skiing brings families and friends together. It makes people feel healthy and happy.

So don't forget that the most important reason to ski is that you enjoy the skiing itself, and the most important reason to improve is that you'll enjoy it more. And if you're happy when you ski, you must be doing something right.

Index

Note: The italicized *f* and *t* following page numbers refer to figures and tables, respectively.

About the Author

Ron LeMaster has spent more than 30 years as a ski instructor and race coach. Certified and accredited by the Professional Ski Instructors of America, LeMaster is a technical advisor to the U.S. Ski Team and Vail Ski School, and he lectures frequently about technique and biomechanics to ski schools and teams around North America, South America, and Europe.

A regular contributor to skiing magazines, LeMaster also has written technical guides for the Professional Ski Instructors of America and contributed to educational materials for the U.S. Coaches Association. He holds degrees in mechanical engineering and computer science.

LeMaster lives in Boulder, Colorado, where he enjoys skiing and cycling.